Part One

MOUNTAIN BIKES

Janet Cook

Consultants: **Al Heubach and Geoff Apps**

Designed by **Mary Forster**

Additional designs by **Ruth Strohl-Palmer**

Cover design by **Stephen Wright**

Illustrated by **Kim Raymond** and **Kuo Kang Chen**

Photographs taken on location in California
by **Mike Powell, Allsport USA**

Additional photographs by **Otto Greule, Jr.** and **W.L. Gillingham**

Part One was produced in association with **MUDDY FOX** 🐾

Contents

2

Using part one

Part One covers all you need to know to become a competent rider, from efficient gear-changing and braking to such advanced skills as bunny-hopping and ditch-jumping.

Budding competitors can find out about events such as observed trials and downhill races. There are tips on how to prepare for a competition and do your best on the day.

Emergency repair panels cover some mechanical problems you may encounter *en-route*. On pages 34-45 there is advice on cleaning and maintaining your bike.

Safety first

You can greatly reduce the chances of being seriously injured in a bicycling accident if you ride cautiously and use your common sense. In addition to this, you should always wear a helmet.

Your head is the most sensitive part of your body. Wearing a helmet could prevent concussion, brain damage, or death.

Helmets needn't be uncomfortable. Modern designs are light and well-ventilated.

Mountain bike etiquette

Unfortunately, mountain biking has been given a bad name by a few thoughtless riders who have shown little care for the countryside or other users. It is therefore important that riders work together to earn back respect for the sport. Without the support of landowners, ramblers, horseriders and so on, tracks open to mountain bikes could become very limited.

Remember:

* Give way to other country-side users.
* Don't drop litter.
* Close gates behind you.
* Be polite and courteous.
* As you approach animals, slow down and give them a wide berth.
* Don't take unnecessary risks.
* Don't be too noisy.
* Don't create a fire hazard.
* Don't skid unnecessarily.

About mountain bikes

Mountain bikes are tough. When ridden skilfully, they can go through ditches and potholes, cope with water and mud, climb near-vertical slopes, and bring you downhill with control and stability.

The picture below shows all the mountain bike parts, and tells you what they are called. If you are thinking about buying a bike yourself, go to pages 32-33 for advice.

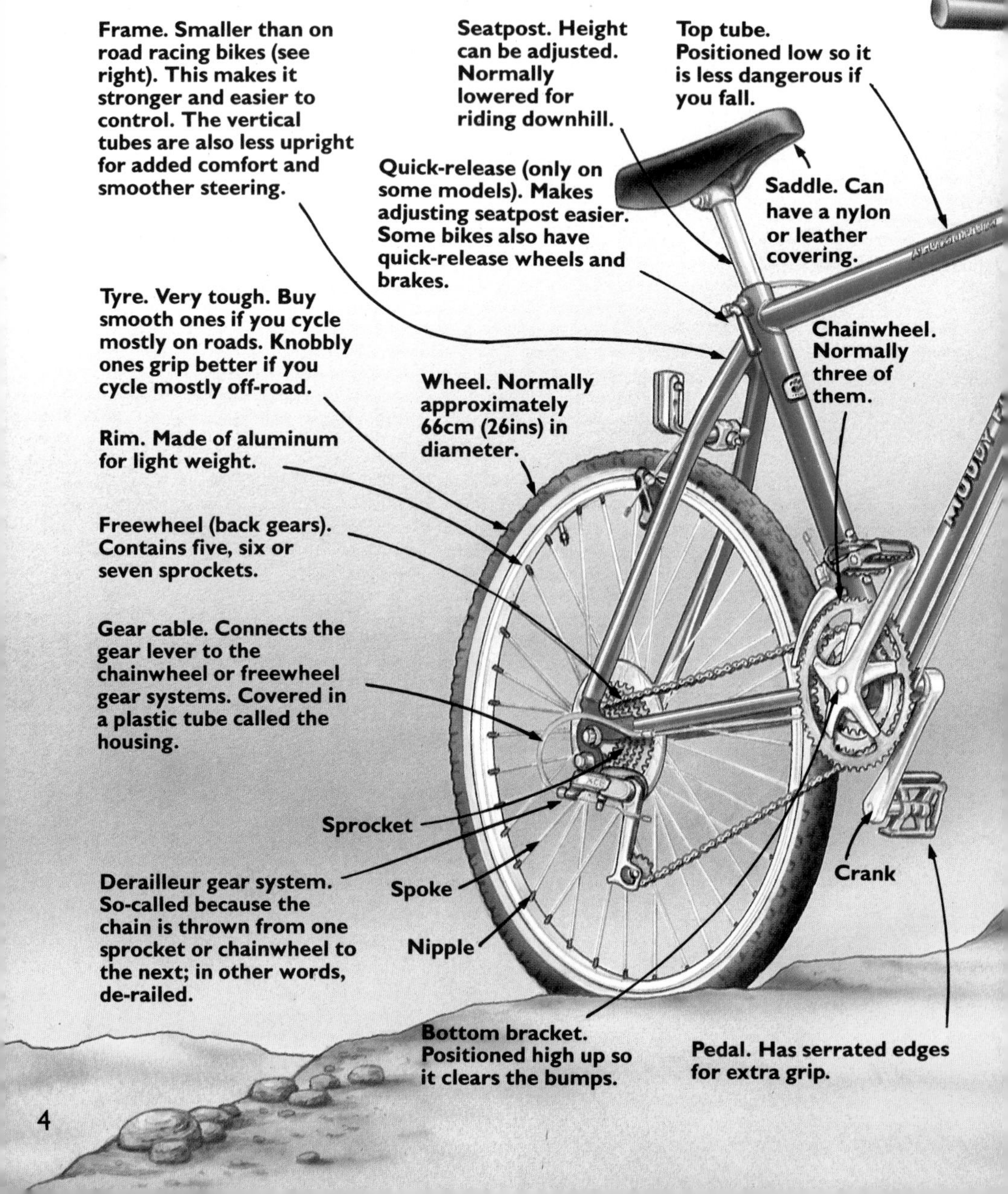

Frame. Smaller than on road racing bikes (see right). This makes it stronger and easier to control. The vertical tubes are also less upright for added comfort and smoother steering.

Seatpost. Height can be adjusted. Normally lowered for riding downhill.

Top tube. Positioned low so it is less dangerous if you fall.

Quick-release (only on some models). Makes adjusting seatpost easier. Some bikes also have quick-release wheels and brakes.

Saddle. Can have a nylon or leather covering.

Tyre. Very tough. Buy smooth ones if you cycle mostly on roads. Knobbly ones grip better if you cycle mostly off-road.

Chainwheel. Normally three of them.

Wheel. Normally approximately 66cm (26ins) in diameter.

Rim. Made of aluminum for light weight.

Freewheel (back gears). Contains five, six or seven sprockets.

Gear cable. Connects the gear lever to the chainwheel or freewheel gear systems. Covered in a plastic tube called the housing.

Sprocket

Derailleur gear system. So-called because the chain is thrown from one sprocket or chainwheel to the next; in other words, de-railed.

Spoke

Nipple

Crank

Bottom bracket. Positioned high up so it clears the bumps.

Pedal. Has serrated edges for extra grip.

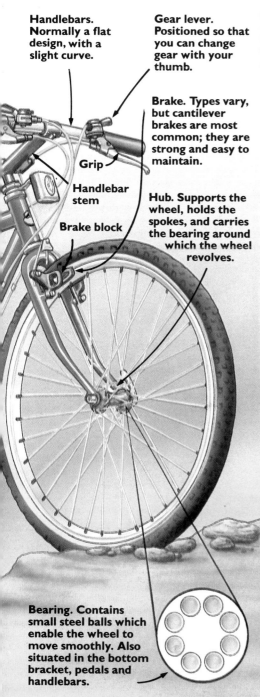

Handlebars. Normally a flat design, with a slight curve.

Gear lever. Positioned so that you can change gear with your thumb.

Brake. Types vary, but cantilever brakes are most common; they are strong and easy to maintain.

Grip

Handlebar stem

Brake block

Hub. Supports the wheel, holds the spokes, and carries the bearing around which the wheel revolves.

Bearing. Contains small steel balls which enable the wheel to move smoothly. Also situated in the bottom bracket, pedals and handlebars.

The first mountain bikes

In the late 1960s, motorcyclists in California, USA, were tearing up the countryside by riding down mountain trails as spectacularly as possible. This was soon banned, but some people were unperturbed. They rode down on tough old bikes instead.

The indestructible 1930s Schwinn Excelsior.

At first, they transported their bikes uphill in pick-up trucks. But then one cycling enthusiast, Gary Fisher, fitted gears to his bike and rode up the steep Repack Hill. By the late 1970s, manufacturers were developing bikes with gears for off-road use. The mountain bike boom had started.

One of the first mountain bikes; the Stumpjumper by Specialized.

Road racing bikes

Mountain bikes are designed for strength and good grip on rough terrain. In contrast, racing bikes are designed for lightness and speed on roads*.

Steep angles provide sensitive steering.

Drop handlebars for perfect racing posture.

Light caliper brakes

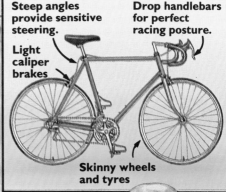

Skinny wheels and tyres

Preparing to go

Before setting out, make sure your bike is roadworthy. Some things to look for are described below. Later on in the book, there is advice on how to do simple repairs.

A bike stand is useful, but not essential. If you don't have one, just rest your bike against a wall.

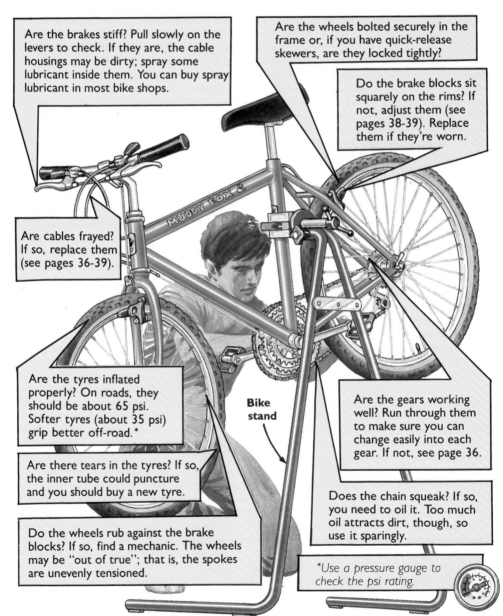

Are the brakes stiff? Pull slowly on the levers to check. If they are, the cable housings may be dirty; spray some lubricant inside them. You can buy spray lubricant in most bike shops.

Are the wheels bolted securely in the frame or, if you have quick-release skewers, are they locked tightly?

Do the brake blocks sit squarely on the rims? If not, adjust them (see pages 38-39). Replace them if they're worn.

Are cables frayed? If so, replace them (see pages 36-39).

Are the tyres inflated properly? On roads, they should be about 65 psi. Softer tyres (about 35 psi) grip better off-road.*

Are there tears in the tyres? If so, the inner tube could puncture and you should buy a new tyre.

Bike stand

Are the gears working well? Run through them to make sure you can change easily into each gear. If not, see page 36.

Does the chain squeak? If so, you need to oil it. Too much oil attracts dirt, though, so use it sparingly.

Do the wheels rub against the brake blocks? If so, find a mechanic. The wheels may be "out of true"; that is, the spokes are unevenly tensioned.

*Use a pressure gauge to check the psi rating.

What to wear

Comfortable clothes can make all the difference between an enjoyable ride and a miserable one. Here are some tips.

Shoes

Mountain bike shoes have stiff soles for comfortable and efficient pedalling, and tough uppers. Cheaper alternatives are lightweight hiking boots, or trainers with thick soles.

Mountain bike shoe

Upper

Stiff sole

Clothes

Several thin layers are better than one thick one; you can take a layer off if you get hot. Avoid trousers with thick seams in the crotch area.

Cotton or polyester and cotton tops help keep you cool.

Padded cycling gloves protect your hands from blisters and scratches. Make sure they fit snugly.

Shorts made from lycra-spandex are like a second skin, and provide good ventilation. The best sort have a padded crotch lining.

Wool keeps you warm even when it's wet. Polypropylene dries quickly and is a good insulator.
   A windcheater is essential in cold weather to protect you from the wind.

*More about helmets on page 77.

Basic tool kit

Take the following items along with you on any ride. Wrap them up in a cloth; you can use this to clean your hands after repairs. Tie them behind your saddle or under the top tube.

Small screwdriver

3, 4, 5 and 6 mm allen keys

Pump

Spare inner tube

Adjustable spanner and crank spanner

Chain tool

Spoke nipple tool

Tyre levers

Swiss army knife

Puncture repair kit

Pliers

Helmets

Most helmets are made of polystyrene, with a plastic and lycra coating. All good ones undergo severe tests for strength and are labelled accordingly.
   Make sure your helmet fits securely and does not interfere with your vision. Test this by putting the helmet on and shaking your head around. It should not flop around or fall forwards*.

Bright helmet for city riding.

Learning the basics

Good braking and gear-changing techniques are essential. Once you have mastered them, you can learn the advanced manoeuvres covered later in this book with greater confidence and control.

A correct riding position is also important. The pictures below show the most efficient and comfortable positions.

Relax your hands and arms.

Bend your arms slightly.

Put the balls of your feet on the pedals.

As you go faster, tuck down and lean forwards.

Keep your hands shoulder-width apart.

Braking

Bad braking techniques could cause you to skid and lose control. Below are the safest techniques. If you feel the bike start to skid, release the front brake.

In wet weather, water between the rims and brake blocks can stop the brakes from working immediately. Because of this, start braking much earlier.

On-road technique

Here you use the front brake as the major force; this prevents the bike from skidding.

1. Put pressure on the front brake, then pull on the back brake too.

2. Increase the pressure on both brakes until the bike stops.

Off-road technique

Here skidding is more likely. A rear wheel skid is easier to control, so you use mainly the back brake.

1. Keeping your weight as far back as possible, ease on the back brake.

2. Make gentle pulls on the front brake (this is called feathering).

Changing gear

Good use of the gears helps you keep the same pedal rate (cadence) throughout the ride. Ideally, this should be 80-90 revolutions per minute; quite a brisk pace.

You have three ranges of gears, as shown below.

The low range consists of the small chainwheel and the two or three largest sprockets. You use these for climbing hills.

The high range is the large chainwheel and the two or three smallest sprockets. These are for fast conditions.

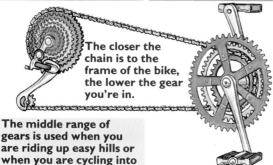

The closer the chain is to the frame of the bike, the lower the gear you're in.

The middle range of gears is used when you are riding up easy hills or when you are cycling into strong winds.

Gear-changing tips

★ Don't use the large chainwheel with the large sprocket, or the small chainwheel with the small sprocket. These are called the cross-over gears. The chain angle is too steep.

★ Ease off the pressure on the pedals when you change gear. This isn't so important in high speed conditions.

★ Use higher gears for cycling on-road than off-road.

Falling off

If you ride carefully, you may never fall. However, if it does happen, you can reduce the chance of hurting yourself if you try to control the fall as shown on the right.*

The key is to keep relaxed. If you are stiff, your body will absorb the full impact of the fall.

1. Imagine yourself cycling at a fast pace (about 20 kmph or 12 mph). The ground ahead of you appears to be free of obstacles.

2. Suddenly you see a large rock in your way. You abruptly turn the handlebars to the left, but your body keeps going forwards.

3. You release your right foot and hand and use them to steady your fall. You use your left ones to ease the bike to the ground.

4. Keeping your arms and legs relaxed to absorb the shock of the fall, you bring your body to a sitting position. No harm is done.

Remember to always wear a helmet.

Don't attempt this unless the fall is unavoidable.

Turning

Mountain bikes are designed for smooth, easy steering. This means that if you use your body-weight correctly, you can master tight curves with ease. However, it is still a good idea to practise turning in flat, quiet areas before facing heavy traffic or bumpy ground.

The basic turn

1. Approach the turn with just enough speed to stop you from wobbling.

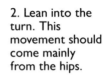

2. Lean into the turn. This movement should come mainly from the hips.

3. Now turn the handlebars as smoothly as you can.

4. Bring the handlebars and your body level again, back on a straight course.

Emergency repair: Broken spoke

1. Remove the wheel and, if it is the back wheel, the freewheel (see page 41).

2. Notice how the broken spoke is threaded through the other spokes. Now unscrew the nipple with a nipple tool and remove the broken spoke.

3. Thread the new spoke on the wheel. Screw in the nipple and tighten it. If necessary, replace the freewheel and back wheel.

4. Spin the wheel. If it hits the brake blocks every so often, tighten the nipple a little more.

Note: If you don't have a spoke with you, just remove the broken one and ride on. Replace it when you get home.

Practising turning

Build a course of large rocks about three metres apart. Now weave between them, varying the speed and sharpness of the turn. Notice that the faster you go, the more you have to lean into the turn.

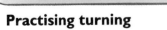

See how slowly you can go.

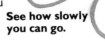

Rock

Sharp turns

If you come across an obstacle unexpectedly, you may need to make a really quick twist around it. The technique below is a good way to do this.

1. Quickly turn the handlebars towards the obstacle, that is, in the opposite direction to the way you want to turn.

2. Immediately turn the handlebars in the direction you want to go. You will be able to make a much sharper turn.

3. When you have got past the obstacle, readjust the handlebars and use your body-weight to coax the bike back on course.

1. Keep up your speed and momentum as you approach the turn.

2. For a left-hand turn, keep the left pedal up as high as it will go.

3. Lean to the left, and push down hard on the right pedal. Gently pull on the back brake.

4. The back wheel will now skid to the right, and try to come round to the front.

Broadslides

Broadslides are performed at moderate to high speeds, and are difficult. Don't try them if you are at all unsure of your ability to control the bike at these speeds.

Because they rely on the bike skidding, you must do them on surfaces with poor traction (grip), such as gravel, grass or dirt. For your first attempts, choose a grassy surface which is free of obstacles.

Although spectacular, this turn can give the impression of irresponsible riding. Don't do it where it may annoy others, or tear up the ground.

5. To counteract the back wheel skid, turn the front wheel gently to the right.

6. Continue leaning to the left and turning the handlebars to the right until the turn is complete.

Going uphill

Riding to the top of a very steep hill is extremely satisfying, and worth all the effort. The advice below will help get you there.

Climbing technique

On steep hills, you should stay in the seat for as long as possible. Your tyres cannot grip the surface so well if you stand, and you may lose momentum. However, on a long, gentle hill you may prefer a variety of sitting, standing and honking (see below).

Sitting position: lean forwards for more controlled steering.

Standing position: concentrate your weight over the pedals.

Honking position: while standing, use your weight to tip the bike from side to side.

Uphill gear-changing

Ideally, you should keep pedalling at the same rate throughout your climb. To do this, choose lower gears than you can manage, and change down before you have to.

Changing gear under pressure could break the gear mechanisms or cause the chain to fall off. The rear gear is particularly sensitive. To avoid this, pedal faster for a short distance, then ease off the pressure as you change up or down.

Tips

★ Look out for rough patches or obstacles, and steer around them.
★ Change up a gear for standing or honking.
★ Rest your hands on the grips whenever possible. This stops your arms and hands getting overtired.
★ If the back wheel starts to slip, slide back on the saddle.
★ If the front wheel lifts up, sit further forward, or stand and lean forwards.
★ If you have both front and back wheel problems, sit further back but lean forwards.
★ For cycling on rough terrain where the tyres find it difficult to grip, let a little air out of them.

Using toe-clips

Many people use toe-clips for climbing. Keep them fairly loose until you are used to them so you can release your feet more easily if you fall.

Pros	Cons
★ It is easy for your feet to slip when you are climbing. Toe-clips secure them to the pedals.	★ You can't use your feet to help you balance, although you can learn to balance without them.
★ They give you extra pedalling power.	★ If you fall, you may not be able to release your feet before you hit the ground.
★ They help you to pedal evenly.	

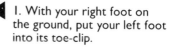

◀ 1. With your right foot on the ground, put your left foot into its toe-clip.

◀ 2. As you move off, position your right foot on its pedal with the toe-clip underneath.

◀ 3. Flick the right pedal over, and slide your foot into the toe-clip.

Carrying your bike

Some hills are too much for anyone to master. In these cases you may need to push or carry your bike before you can get in the saddle again. The following technique is the most efficient and energy-saving way to carry your bike.

Top tube over right shoulder.

Hold the left handlebar.

Emergency repair: Broken chain

1. Use the chain tool to remove one complete link and the pin of the broken link.

2. Snap the ends of the chain together.

3. Push the pin through with the chain tool, bending the chain slightly if the link is stiff.

Note: If the whole chain is worn, buy a new one.

13

Going downhill

One of the most exhilarating experiences on a mountain bike is riding down a steep slope at full pelt. However, at very fast speeds you could seriously hurt yourself, or others, if you lose control. For this reason, never ride recklessly or irresponsibly.

Downhill posture

The trick is to keep your weight low and to the back of the bike, as shown below. Lowering the saddle position will help you to do this (see page 35).

If you lean forwards, you are likely to be catapulted over the handlebars.

Before setting off, check your brakes, and make sure your tyres are firm.

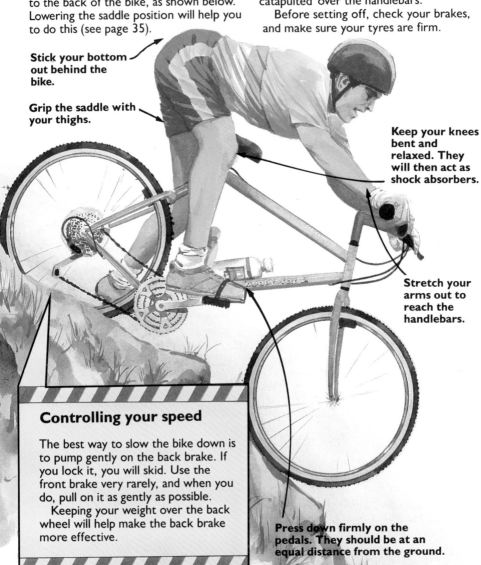

Stick your bottom out behind the bike.

Grip the saddle with your thighs.

Keep your knees bent and relaxed. They will then act as shock absorbers.

Stretch your arms out to reach the handlebars.

Controlling your speed

The best way to slow the bike down is to pump gently on the back brake. If you lock it, you will skid. Use the front brake very rarely, and when you do, pull on it as gently as possible.

Keeping your weight over the back wheel will help make the back brake more effective.

Press down firmly on the pedals. They should be at an equal distance from the ground.

Steering around obstacles

On a fast downhill stretch, an unexpected obstacle such as a rock or log may make you turn the handlebars too sharply and lose control. If you see something ahead, follow these steps.

1. Try to slow the bike down, pulling gently on both brakes. Keep your weight to the back of the bike.

2. Lean your body in the direction of the turn. Now ease the handlebars round as gently as you can.

3. For maximum ground clearance, position the pedal nearest the obstacle as high as possible.

4. Finally, lean outwards to bring the bike level again.

Emergency repair: Punctures

1. Remove the wheel (see page 41). Now, starting opposite the valve, remove one side of the tyre from the rim.

2. Remove the inner tube then inflate it. Listen for a hiss or put the tube in water and watch for bubbles. Mark the hole.

3. Use fine sandpaper to roughen area around the hole. Blow away any dust. Spread glue on the area. Leave for two minutes.

4. Stick on the patch then let it dry for three minutes. Check in the tyre for grit.

5. Starting with the valve, replace the tube, then the tyre, on the rim. Make sure it is tucked in all the way. Pump up the tyre.

Mountain bike slalom

Just as skiers sometimes take a zig-zag course (slalom) to go down mountains, this can be a good way to ride down very steep slopes. It enables you to go slower as the descent is less severe.

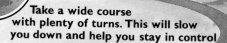

Use a broadslide (see page 10) to change direction in an emergency.

Take a wide course with plenty of turns. This will slow you down and help you stay in control

Wheelies

A wheelie involves pulling the front wheel in the air and balancing on the back one alone. It is a good way to impress friends as it looks trickier than it really is. It is also useful for getting over obstacles.

The basic technique

Practise the basic wheelie technique on a clear area of soft ground, such as grass. Make sure you wear padded clothing to protect you in case you fall.

1. Get into a low gear and ride along at an easy pace.

2. Bring your weight directly over the back of the bike.

3. Pull the handlebars up and back and push down hard on the pedals.

4. To recover, bring your body-weight forward again.

Key pointers

★ Really yank at the handlebars. If you're too gentle, the front wheel will scarcely rise and will quickly fall down again.

★ Keep your weight directly over the point where the back wheel touches the ground. If it's further back, you will topple backwards; any further forwards, and the front wheel will hardly move.

Emergency repair: Dented rim

1. Remove the wheel (see page 41 to find out how to remove a back wheel). Place it on a flat surface.

2. Use a hammer, rock, or block of wood to flatten the dent. Use your other hand to keep the wheel steady.

3. Reassemble the bike. When you get home, take the wheel to a bike shop. They will do a permanent repair with specialist tools, or replace the whole wheel.

Note: Only do this if the dent is badly affecting the brakes; you could split the rim altogether.

Using a wheelie over obstacles

Although top riders can wheelie over obstacles of around one metre, most people are content to master obstacles of around 30cm. Practise at first with a small log or rock. Secure it by digging it slightly into the ground. Now position yourself about 50m away.

 1. Slowly ride towards the log in a low gear.

2. Just before you reach the log, stand up and bring your weight back.

3. Now use a wheelie (see left) to pull the front wheel over the log.

4. Bring your weight forwards to stop the wheelie from going too far. Pedal hard to pull the back wheel over the log too.

Doing a wheelie uphill

If you do a normal wheelie while going uphill you could well fall backwards. Instead, bend your arms and lower your chest as you lift the handlebars. This is called down-unweighting. It will help you over obstacles on your way up.

Don't try this on a steep hill.

You won't lose much speed, so carry on up the hill afterwards.

Doing a wheelie downhill

This is very difficult. If you don't keep your weight back, you could fly over the handlebars. If you do try one, go to a gentle slope. If you feel you're losing control, try to bring the wheel back down again and gently pull on the brakes to reduce your speed.

Ease the bike back to the ground again very gently.

Bunny-hopping

A bunny-hop is an extension of a wheelie. After lifting up the front wheel, you raise the back one too.

You are less likely to damage your bike if you use a bunny-hop to get over obstacles. This is because the back wheel hops over obstacles, rather than hitting them.

◀ 1. Follow the instructions on page 16 to lift the front wheel in the air.

Bunny-hopping tips

★ Both techniques on this page need lots of practice. Don't worry if you can't master them straight away.
★ The key to good bunny-hopping is to shift your weight as abruptly and forcefully as you can.
★ Wearing toe clips makes the double wheel technique much easier.

2. Bring your weight forwards, while pushing down and back on the pedals. ▶

3. The front wheel will hit the ground and the back wheel will rise. ▶

Double wheel technique

A double wheel bunny-hop is when you lift both wheels off the ground simultaneously. Here is how you do it:

1. Ride along slowly on level ground. Stay out of the saddle, and keep your feet level. ▼

2. Quickly push down on the handlebars and pedals, then pull the whole bike upwards. ▼

4. Start pedalling so that the bike clears the obstacle, then bring your weight back over the centre of the bike. ▶

Jumping

Full-scale jumps are fun but dangerous. Protect yourself from potential falls by wearing clothes that are well padded (especially on your knees and elbows) and, as always, a strong helmet.

1. Keep your speed up as you approach the area you want to jump.

An off-road track can be precarious, especially if you haven't ridden it before. For example, the ground could suddenly drop in front of you. Alternatively, you could face a deep ditch. A jump is often the best solution.

Jumping a sudden drop in ground level.

Jumping a deep ditch.

2. Take off, then use your weight to balance the bike. Keep all your movements as smooth as possible.

3. If you start to wobble, grip the saddle tightly with your thighs.

Coping with bomb-holes

Some holes (called bomb-holes) are too big to jump. On the right you can see how to ride through one. This is also a good technique to use when you are going too slowly to jump a ditch.

1. Enter the bomb-hole at speed, with your weight well back. At the bottom, bend your knees, and down-unweight.

2. Pedal fast to gain momentum. As you ascend, stop pedalling and bring your weight forward and up.

4. Use your weight to make the rear wheel land slightly before the front one.

19

Riding on difficult surfaces

Mountain bikes are designed to cope with extreme conditions, including water, mud, sand, ice and snow. However, you do need to adapt your riding technique in order to stay in control of your bike in these conditions. Below are some tips on how to do this.

Before the crossing

★ Inspect the stream carefully:

1. How deep is it? If it's higher than your bottom bracket, you'll end up swimming rather than riding through it.

2. Are there many boulders? If so, try to find a smoother part of the stream.

3. Is the current strong? If so, don't risk it.

★ Lower the seat of your bike (see page 34). This will make you more stable.

★ Loosen your toe straps. You may need to remove your feet in a hurry if you lose your balance.

★ Make sure all the nuts and bolts are done up tightly.

Crossing water

The secret of crossing shallow streams and creeks is to pedal extra hard so you keep going at a fast speed. Your momentum will then carry you over rocks and other obstacles in your way.

1. Approach the stream as quickly as possible. Lean forwards as you enter.

2. Transfer your weight to the back of the bike. This makes it easier for the front wheel to get over rocks and so on.

3. Keep pedalling all the way through if you can. This will help you keep your balance and momentum.

Mud, snow, sand and ice

Riding on these treacherous surfaces requires a lot of common sense. In particular, keep away from melting ice, and avoid cycling in deep snow (10cm or 4 ins is about the limit). Also, never cycle on these surfaces if there are other vehicles present; they could easily lose control and skid into you.

Make sure you clean your bike thoroughly afterwards (see page 35).

	Potential problems	Preparation	Riding tips
Mud and snow	★ Riding fast enough to avoid sinking. ★ Steering. ★ Skidding when climbing. ★ Mud clogging up parts or gear cables freezing.	★ Protect your eyes with fitted glasses. ★ Use knobbly tyres inflated to about 35 psi. ★ Take spray lubricant. It may help free frozen gears.	★ Pedal quickly in a low gear. ★ Brake very gently. ★ Steer smoothly. An abrupt turn will cause the front wheel to plough sideways.
Sand	★ Sand on the chain makes it hard to change gear. ★ Sinking. ★ Sand flying in your face.	★ Wear glasses, and wrap a scarf around your face. ★ Don't alter tyre pressure or tread; no tyres grip sand.	★ Stay in a low gear to avoid sinking. ★ Steer very gently. ★ Distribute your weight evenly across the bike.
Ice	★ Skidding. ★ Parts freezing up. ★ Falling off can cause serious injury. Avoid cycling in ice if possible.	★ Use spray lubricant on frozen parts. ★ Neither tyre pressure nor grip make a difference.	★ Go just fast enough to balance. ★ No abrupt moves. ★ If you skid, steer into the skid.

4. Keep your weight over the back wheel as the front wheel climbs out of the stream.

Emergency repair: Loose crank

1. Put the chain on the largest chainwheel. Remove dust cap from the crank.

2. Tighten the bolt by fitting the crank spanner over it and turning clockwise. For leverage, press down on opposite pedal with other hand.

3. Replace the dust cap.

Cycling in a city

City cycling presents quite different hazards from those you encounter off-road. These pages will help you prepare for and deal with some of them. Also, ask at your local police station for details about courses on road safety.

You can use smooth tyres because traction isn't a problem. These will give you a much more comfortable ride, especially if you pump them up hard.

Getting to know the route

It is important to know where you are going. Trying to map-read at the side of the road or follow signposts *en route* prevents you from concentrating on the traffic.

Before your ride, take the time to study your route on a detailed map. You may find it helpful to write yourself brief notes, then memorize them.

Cycle the route slowly, looking out for danger areas. You will then be fully prepared next time.

* North up City Road
* 4th right Hoskins Street
* Approx 5 Kilometres — roundabout.
2nd left Park Row.
* 3rd left Kestrel Street
* 1st right Cherry Tree Rd.
* 2nd right East Welling Avenue

Coping with fumes

Traffic fumes can make city cycling unpleasant and unhealthy. Because you are close to the exhaust pipes, you breathe in carbon monoxide and other chemicals in a concentrated form. You also inhale more as you are breathing harder and faster than normal.

You could buy a mask, but this will only filter out grit. Try to avoid cycling in rush-hour traffic when fumes are dense, and take back roads when possible.

Dressing to be seen

Because your bike is much smaller and quieter than other traffic, it is essential that you do everything you can to draw attention to yourself. Use your lights whenever visibility is bad, not just at night-time.

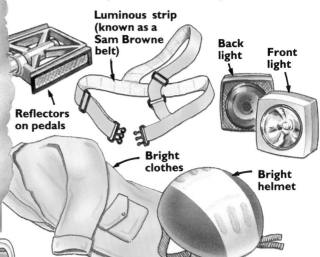

Luminous strip (known as a Sam Browne belt)

Back light

Front light

Reflectors on pedals

Bright clothes

Bright helmet

Traffic hazards

Cycling in traffic requires you to cope with situations where other people act stupidly. Below are some things to look out for.

People opening their car doors or pulling out right in front of you.

Motorcyclists (particularly despatch riders) swerving in and out of cars.

Drivers cutting you off as they make a turn into a side road or driveway.

Safety tips

Do:

★ Make clear hand signals.
★ Use a bell, horn or whistle to let others (especially pedestrians) know you're there.
★ Keep looking behind. It's easier to duck your head than twist your neck right round.
★ Keep your hands on the brake levers, ready to brake at a moment's notice.
★ Watch out if it starts to rain. The road will be very slippery then and you can lose about 50% of your braking power.
★ Give parked cars a wide berth.

Don't:

★ Jump red or amber traffic lights.
★ Cycle on pavements or the wrong way up one-way streets.
★ Cycle if you have been drinking alcohol. This is dangerous and illegal.
★ Go too slowly; you will frustrate others and make them act stupidly.
★ Cycle too close to the car in front.

Cycling over pot-holes

The best way to deal with pot-holes is to steer round them. However, the flow of traffic may make this impossible. Below you can see how to ride over them safely. Alternatively, do a bunny-hop (see page 18).

1. Slow down, then get into a standing position with your knees bent.

2. Grip the handlebars firmly, keeping your arms relaxed and your weight well back.

3. Keep the bike straight and pull up on the handlebars as you go through the pot-hole.

4. Pick up speed again once the back wheel is clear.

Locking up

You can reduce the chances of your bike being stolen by locking it securely. Take any removable parts (such as the saddle) with you.

Write your name and post code on the bike in indelible ink.

Detach the front wheel (if it is QR) and lock it with the back wheel and frame to a lamp-post, using a steel lock.

Planning an expedition

The secret of a successful cycling trip is thorough planning. Below are some tips on how to prepare for your expedition.

Researching the area

Once you have decided where you would like to go, you need to spend some time finding out what conditions you can expect. As well as making use of guidebooks, there are a number of experts you should talk to.

Question	Who to ask?
1. What will the weather be like? Hot/Cold? Dry/Wet? Humid? Stormy? Windy?	1. Local weather centre
2. What sort of extra equipment should I take to cope with the conditions?	2. Local bicycle shop (check cycling magazines for shops in the area).
3. What accommodation is available in the area? Do I need to book in advance?	3. Local tourist office
4. Are there any potential problem areas? Are there any safer routes I could opt for if necessary?	4. Local bicycle shop or a cycling organization (see page 46). They may put you in touch with someone who knows the area.

Packing your bike

You need to keep your bike as light as possible while ensuring you have the essentials. Here are the basics; you may need to take some extras suited to the terrain.

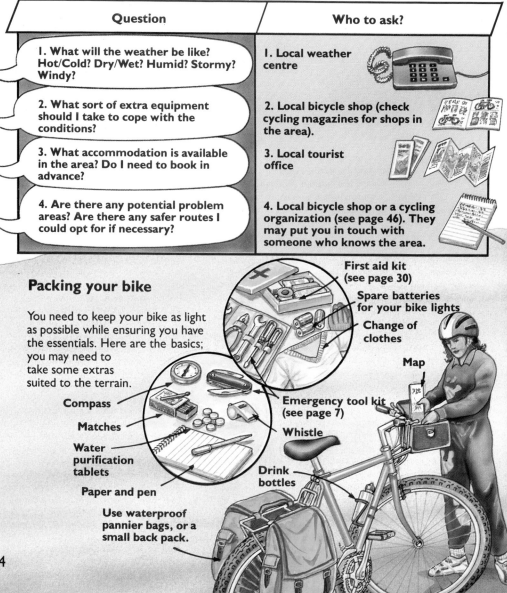

First aid kit (see page 30)

Spare batteries for your bike lights

Change of clothes

Map

Emergency tool kit (see page 7)

Whistle

Compass

Matches

Water purification tablets

Paper and pen

Drink bottles

Use waterproof pannier bags, or a small back pack.

Training

It is a mistake to start cycling very long distances without a proper build-up.

Adapt the basic training programme shown below to suit your capabilities.

	WEEK 1	WEEK 2			WEEK 3	WEEK 4
MON	8 Km easy	12 Km easy		MON	15 Km easy	25 Km easy
TUES	8 Km easy	12 Km easy		TUES	15 Km easy	25 Km hard
WED	12 Km easy	12 Km easy		WED	15 Km easy	25 Km easy
THURS	12 Km easy	12 Km easy		THURS	15 Km hard	25 Km hard
FRI	8 Km easy	15 Km easy		FRI	15 Km easy	25 Km easy
SAT	25 Km easy	30 Km easy		SAT	50 Km easy	65 Km easy
SUN	OFF	OFF		SUN	OFF	

Roof-rack or boot-rack?

If you want to transport your bike by car, you will need a bike rack.

Roof-racks can carry up to five bikes. You can buy attachments which enable them to carry other sports gear. They are expensive.

Most **boot-racks** can carry two bikes. They are easier to use, and a fraction of the price.

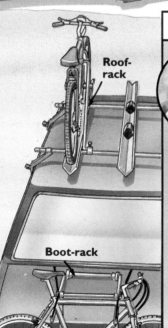

Roof-rack

Boot-rack

Going abroad

If you plan to go abroad, ask a travel agent whether you need any visas. Also find out whether you need medical supplies such as diarrhoea tablets, or if you should have any injections.

As well as learning some of the language, find out about the local customs. It is easy to cause offence through the way you dress or behave.

The expedition itself

Even the most well-planned expedition could become a total disaster if you don't look after yourselves and each other on the way. These two pages will provide you with some useful advice.

Cycling as a team

It is vital that the stronger cyclists in the group watch out for the weaker ones and alter their riding pace if it is necessary. Use the tips on the right to make sure the whole group works well together.

Food and drink

In the first few hours of cycling, your energy comes from glycogen stored in the muscles and liver. Your body makes glycogen from carbohydrates in food. There are many good sources of carbohydrates; a few are shown below. By eating them before and during the trip, you can improve your cycling performance dramatically.

Fresh vegetables

Fresh fruit

Rice

Pasta

On-ride snacks

"The bonk" is a common problem. It happens when you have used up your glycogen, and have no energy left. To avoid this, eat snacks (such as energy bars or dried fruit) regularly *en-route*.

Energy bars are packed with carbohydrates. Buy them from cycle shops.

You can use up a lot of liquid through sweating. Drink frequently so you don't get dehydrated.

Team tips

★ Work out a realistic plan for the day which you are all happy with. Be ready to alter it if someone gets tired.

★ Put a strong cyclist at the back of the group. It is demoralising for a slow cyclist to struggle at the back.

★ Don't wait for someone to admit they're tired. They may not want to hold up the rest of the group.

★ If you are cycling into a strong wind, take turns at the front of the group.

★ If you have touring gear, the strongest cyclist should carry the heavier items.

Safety tips

★ Check your equipment daily (see page 6) and listen for rattles or squeaks *en-route*.

★ Always wear a shirt; riding without one speeds up dehydration.

★ Let someone know your plans each day. Contact them again in the evening when you have arrived safely.

★ If you are hit by very bad weather, take the shortest route to civilisation and ask for help. If visibility is bad, find a sheltered place and stay put.

If it is cold, huddle together.

Weather watch

By watching out for rain, you can take shelter before it arrives. Listen to the forecast before you set off, and look for the tell-tale signs below. If you do get drenched, change into dry clothes immediately. If it is very cold, put wet items in a plastic bag at the bottom of your sleeping bag to stop them freezing.

Red sky first thing in the morning.

Low clouds which haven't cleared by midday.

Cumulonimbus clouds mean storms are coming.

Lightning

The metal in your bike attracts lightning and is potentially very dangerous. If you get caught in a lightning storm, abandon your bike and head for shelter. Avoid high ground or trees; lightning looks for the shortest route to earth, and either of these may be its target.

Entering a competiton

You don't have to be a top rider to enter a mountain bike competition. Unlike road racing, you are competing against the terrain just as much as against other cyclists. It is a perfect opportunity to watch others and pick up tips from them.

You can often enter just by turning up on the day. However, many races have number restrictions, so it is safer to send off an entry form in advance. These are available from the race organization, bike shops and magazines.

Types of competition

There are four main types of competition, described below.

Cross-country racing. Competitors race over a course which contains sharp turns, obstacles to jump, streams, steep hills and so on. The cyclist who gets to the finish line first is the winner.

Downhills and slalom. Cyclists ride at top speed down a hair-raising hill. The start is normally staggered (that is, riders start one at a time). The cyclist with the best time wins.

Hill-climbs. Cyclists climb a steep hill, negotiating rocks, loose dirt and so on. Normally a staggered start, the winner is either the one with the best time, or who climbs the highest.

Observed trials. Competitors ride over obstacles, watched by judges. The aim is to get no points. You score one if you touch the ground (dab), three for numerous dabs and five for a fall or a stop.

Preparing to race

Three main things affect your racing performance: your fitness, energy, and the condition of your bike. By concentrating on improving each of these, you will greatly increase your chances of success.

1. Fitness. How fit you are largely depends on your training schedule. Aim to include both long-distance road cycling (for endurance) and off-road challenges, such as climbing and jumping (for strength and technique).

2. Energy. This largely depends on your diet. You can build up your energy stores by eating food which is high in carbohydrates (see page 26). To preserve your energy, only train lightly the day before the race.

3. Bike. If anything goes wrong with your bike during a race, you must fix it on your own. It is vital that you check your bike at least a day before the race, and carry a puncture repair kit and pump during the race.

Race day tips

START

If you are allowed to, pre-ride the course to get familiar with the difficult parts. Then at least you'll know what to expect.

Try to get a good start (if it is a mass start, the front bikes kick up mud and dust on those behind).

If you want to overtake riders, warn them, then wait for them to respond before trying to get past.

You must move over quickly if a racer warns you he or she is about to overtake.

If you get a puncture, fix it and get going as quickly as possible. Some people carry small carbon dioxide cartridges with them which inflate the tyre in seconds.

Don't try to be flashy by jumping higher than necessary; the bike is only in control when on the ground.

FINISH

Iditabike

This is one of the most gruelling races invented. Cyclists ride a 320km (200 mile) course in Alaska in winter. Temperatures drop to 20°C, giving many riders frostbite and even causing tyres to deflate.

Injuries

You can avoid most cycling injuries by taking a few simple precautions. However, the odd ache or graze is unavoidable; below is advice on how to treat them. For more serious injuries, see your doctor.

Warming up and down

You can often avoid getting aching muscles by doing a few light exercises before and after the ride. This is particularly important before and after a race. Some good ones are shown below.

Always start the ride gently, gradually building up as your muscles loosen. Ease off the pace as you cycle home.

Don't be tempted to coast down hills. By pedalling, you help your muscles to recover from the stress of intense effort, and keep the blood circulating.

Knee lunges: keeping your right leg straight, lunge to the left for ten seconds. Go back to the standing position, then lunge to the right. Repeat five times.

Arm rotations: Stretch your arms out either side of you. Now rotate them forwards ten times, then backwards ten times. Repeat five times.

Toe touches: With feet apart and legs straight, touch your left foot with your right hand, then your right foot with your left hand. Do ten times.

First aid kit

Aim to include at least the following items in your kit:

* ★ Large triangular bandage (for slings)
* ★ Sterile dressings
* ★ Roll of bandage
* ★ Elastic bandage
* ★ Plasters
* ★ Aspirin
* ★ Antiseptic lotion
* ★ Cleansing wipes
* ★ Insect repellant
* ★ Scissors
* ★ Tweezers
* ★ Safety pins

Making an ice pack

You can relieve an aching limb by holding an ice pack against it for about 20 minutes. You can buy ice packs from large chemists. Alternatively, use a packet of frozen peas, or make a home-made ice pack shown below. Always keep a towel between the ice pack and limb to avoid ice burns.

Alcohol prevents the mixture from freezing.

1. Mix together some water and medicinal alcohol (available from chemists).

2. Pour into a container. Label it.

3. Put in the freezer. When you need it, pour into a waterproof bag.

Injury chart

Problem	Cause	Solution
Stiff neck	Wearing a heavy helmet, lack of head movement, or over-stretched riding position.	Rotate your head from time to time or buy a lighter helmet. Lower saddle or move it forwards (see page 35).
Stitch	Lack of oxygen getting to muscles, and overworking the diaphragm through quick, shallow breathing.	Reduce cycling pace. Practise taking deeper breaths from the abdomen rather than the chest.
Blisters or numb hands	Gripping the handlebars too tightly or too much weight on the wrists because handlebars are too low or too far forward.	Wear padded cycling gloves or use a more padded grip. Vary hand position on long rides. Adjust handlebars (see pages 44-45).
Stiff knees	Cycling in too high a gear, or for too long. Alternatively, a too low or high saddle.	Reduce gear and build up distance gradually. Set seat to proper height (see page 35).
Numb feet	Wearing tight shoes, or using tight toe straps.	Buy new shoes, or loosen toe straps.
Cramp	Cycling too hard without proper training, or not drinking enough.	Gently rub area. Build up cycling distances/intensity gradually. Drink regularly when cycling.
Aching buttocks	Using a hard saddle, or cycling too far without a build-up.	Buy a new saddle or wear padded trousers or shorts.
Cuts and grazes	On-ride falls or scrapes	Clean with running water then disinfect. Stop a deep cut from bleeding by dressing it tightly, and covering with a thick bandage.
Sprain or pulled muscle	Falling or moving awkwardly	Press an ice-pack against it, then bandage and rest.
Headache, light-headedness or wheezy chest.	Dehydration	Stop cycling, and drink fluid. Rest in the shade and if you have enough water, pour some on your head.

Buying a mountain bike

There are so many mountain bikes on the market that it is easy to get confused when buying one. Below is advice on how to make sure you end up with a bike that is good value and will last you for some time.

Finding a good shop

If you decide to buy a brand-new bike, it is worthwhile looking for a good specialist shop that will not only give you sound advice on your purchase, but will also supply you with back-up mechanical help when you need it. Go to several shops, preferably when they are not too busy (winter is ideal). Look out for the following things:

★ Do they have a good selection?
★ Are the salespeople answering their customers' queries intelligently and courteously? Are they pushy?

★ How do the prices compare with other shops?
★ Do they have a service area with mechanics who can modify bikes to suit their customers' needs?
★ Do they offer free services with the purchase of a bike, such as a year's free maintenance?

Don't consider buying a bike from any shop which fails to impress you on all these counts. Also, ask friends and neighbours whether the shop has a good reputation.

Narrowing it down

To narrow down your choice of bikes, you need to ask yourself the following questions:

★ Will I ride it mostly on- or off-road?
★ What is my price limit?
★ Do I want to race on it?

The test ride

Now take your favourite bike for a short ride in a quiet area. Do the following tests:

★ If you can, take both hands off the handlebars. Does the bike continue in a straight line?
★ Try out all the gears. Are the changes smooth?

★ Try a few emergency stops. How good are the brakes?
★ Does the bike fit you; do you feel cramped, or are you reaching for the handlebars and pedals (see right)?

Before making a decision to buy the bike, take out a few other bikes for test rides to compare their performances.

The final adjustments

The salesperson should now fine-tune the bike to make it perfect for you. This includes getting the fit right, and adding any accessories that you want.

Buying second-hand

Used bikes can be excellent value for money if you know what to look for. It is worth getting the advice of an experienced rider or mechanic before putting your money on the table. Also, check the cost of similar new bikes to make sure the second-hand price is reasonable.

Places to look

1. Phone up local bike shops to find out whether they stock used bikes. Many overhaul used bikes, and sell them with a guarantee.

2. Check bike shops for notice boards. These often advertise used bikes.
3. Look in the classified sections of cycling magazines.

Inspecting the bike

A used bike is bound to have taken some knocks in its time. However, you should look out for major signs of damage or wear such as those described below.
If you are confident that the bike is roadworthy, take it for a test ride.

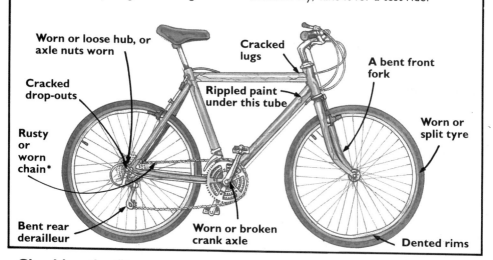

Worn or loose hub, or axle nuts worn

Cracked lugs

A bent front fork

Cracked drop-outs

Rippled paint under this tube

Rusty or worn chain*

Worn or split tyre

Bent rear derailleur

Worn or broken crank axle

Dented rims

Checking the fit

When you buy a second-hand bike, you alone are responsible for making sure it fits you correctly. Check the following:

1. Are the seatpost and handlebar stem long enough for you to set the saddle and handlebars at the right height?**
2. Straddle the bike. For city riding, there should be at least 3-5cm (1-2 ins) between your crotch and top tube; twice that for off-road riding.

3. Can you reach the handlebars while keeping your elbows slightly bent?

Never buy a bike that doesn't fit you:

★ Low handlebars make you lean too far forward, causing a stiff neck and sore back.
★ A badly-positioned saddle can give you knee, hip and ankle problems.
★ If the top tube is too high, you could get very painful injuries in a fall.

*This will mean renewing the chainwheels and sprockets as well as the chain.
**See pages 35 and 45 for more about this.

Maintenance 1: General

If you want to get the most out of your bike, you need to take good care of it. The following twelve pages will help you do just that.

Don't worry if many of the parts shown in the photographs aren't exactly the same as those on your bike. There are lots of different makes and models of bike, but they all work in a similar way.

Cleaning your bike

Cleaning your bike stops mud from building up, and makes it run better. It also lets you inspect the bike more closely.
After a muddy ride, give it a quick clean before the mud has time to dry. Clean it thoroughly two or three times a year.

Post-ride clean

You will need:

Garden hose
2 clean old towels
An old, medium-sized paintbrush
Spray lubricant, such as WD40

1. Use the hose and brush to remove mud. Don't jet water at the headset*, bottom bracket** and pedals; dirty water damages the bearings.
2. Wipe the bike. Clean the moving parts and chain with lubricant, avoiding brake blocks and rims.

Thorough clean

You will need:
Garden hose
2 buckets
1 shallow metal tray
2 sponges
3 rags or old towels
1 stiff brush
1 soft brush
Liquid detergent
Tooth brush
White spirit *
Good quality car wax*
Piece of steel wool
   (medium texture) *
Chain tool **
Chain oil **
Touch-up paint**
Spray lubricant*
Spanner (if wheels
   aren't QR)

* Available from a
   hardware store
** Available from
   a bicycle shop.

1. Spray off most of the mud with a hose.
2. Place your bike on a repair stand, or place it upside-down on a flat area. Use a towel to protect it from scuffs.
3. Remove the wheels (see page 40).
4. Break the chain with a chain tool (see page 13), put it in a shallow tin, and cover with white spirit. Use the toothbrush to scrub off the worst grime, then replace the dirty white spirit with clean spirit. Leave the chain soaking.
5. Wipe the chainwheels with a towel, then clean the freewheel sprockets with the firm brush.
6. Turn the frame the right way up, and rest it on the front forks and chainwheels.
7. Mix detergent and hot water in a bucket. Clean the frame and wheels with this, using the soft brush. Rinse with a hose, avoiding the bearing parts (see above).
8. Remove any rust from the frame with wire wool. Touch up with paint and allow several hours to dry.
9. Rub wax into the frame, then polish it off when dry.
10. Hold the chain above the tray, and let the spirit drip from it until it's dry.
11. Turn the frame upside-down again and replace the wheels. Put the chain on and join with a chain tool.
12. With the bike the right way up, spray lubricant on the chain, gears and brake pivots. Avoid getting any on the rims or blocks, or the brakes won't work.

34   *See page 44.
**See page 42.

Checking the saddle height

A badly-positioned saddle can cause you a great deal of pain (see page 31). Do the following test to see if you need to alter the height of your saddle.

Using a wall to help you balance, sit on the bike and position the pedal at its lowest position. Now put your foot on it. Your leg should be slightly bent (see right).

Correct height   **Incorrect height**

Adjusting the height

The way you adjust the saddle height depends on whether you have a quick-release or bolt-on saddle. In either case, you should leave at least 6.5cm (2.5 ins) of stem inside the frame so it is held securely.

Quick-release (QR) saddles: open the QR lever and raise or lower the saddle. If it's stiff, twist it at the same time. Close the QR lever and check that it's tight.

QR lever

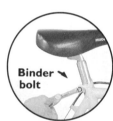
Binder bolt

Bolt-on saddles: use a spanner or allen key to undo the binder bolt. Raise or lower the saddle, twisting it as you do so if it's stiff. Tighten the binder bolt firmly.

Tool kit

To do the maintenance repairs covered on the next few pages, you will need the following items:

Brake cables
Gear cables
Spoke nipple tool
Allen keys
Screwdrivers
Plastic-ended hammer
Pliers
Spray lubricant
Cable cutters
Torch
Spare brake blocks
Bearings
Hook spanner
Bicycle grease
Adjustable spanner
Pin tool
Cotterless crank removing tool
Chain tool
Headset spanner
Freewheel remover
Cone spanner
Rags
Small spanner

Maintenance tips

★ Good tools last longer and make the job easier. To save money, buy jointly with a friend.
★ Clean tools with a rag when you have finished, and store them in a box.
★ Spread paper under the bike to soak up oil or catch dirt.
★ Whenever you dismantle a part, lay out the pieces in the order they came off, and watch carefully so that you can reassemble it correctly.
★ Study your owner's manual (if you have one) before starting.
★ Look up unfamilar technical terms in the glossary on page 47.

There is nothing more frustrating than trying to get up a hill, only to find that your gears fail you. Skilful gear-changing and regular maintenance will help prevent this from happening.

How they work

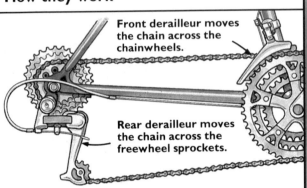

Front derailleur moves the chain across the chainwheels.

Rear derailleur moves the chain across the freewheel sprockets.

The derailleurs do just what they say they do: they derail the chain. When you move the right gear lever, the rear derailleur shifts the chain from one freewheel sprocket to another. When you move the left gear lever, the front derailleur moves the chain from one chainwheel to another.

Derailleur height

Put the chain on the middle chainwheel. There should be 2mm between the outer plate of the front derailleur and the teeth of the largest chainwheel.

Outer plate

If the front derailleur is too high or low, it may not control the chain effectively. Correct this by loosening the clamp bolt and moving the derailleur up or down. Retighten the bolt firmly.

Derailleur alignment

Sometimes a derailleur gets knocked so that it sits at an angle to the sprockets or chainwheels. This stops it from working smoothly and efficiently. Check both derailleurs regularly, particularly after a bad fall, and if necessary correct them as follows:

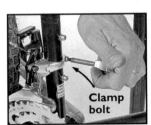

Clamp bolt

If the rear derailleur isn't aligned with the freewheel sprockets, gently pull it into position with a large adjustable spanner.

If the front derailleur isn't aligned, undo the clamp bolt. Reset derailleur then retighten the bolt while holding the derailleur.

Replacing a cable

When a cable starts to fray or rust, it is a sure sign that it will snap before long. If you inspect your cables regularly, and replace them when necessary, you can avoid the possibility of one snapping just when you most need it.

If one gear cable looks worn, think about replacing the other one too. It is probably coming to the end of its life.

Notice that the cable is made up of an inner wire running through a flexible plastic casing (housing).

Overshifting and undershifting

A common derailleur problem is that the chain overshoots the smallest or largest sprocket or chainwheel. This is called overshifting. Alternatively, it may be impossible to move the chain into the smallest or largest sprocket or chainwheel. This is undershifting.

There are two screws on the rear derailleur, called the high and low adjustment screws. These control how far the derailleur moves the chain across the sprockets when you change gear.

At the top of the front derailleur are the inside and outside limit screws. These control how far the derailleur moves the chain across the chainwheels.

Rear derailleur

Turn high adjustment screw* clockwise if the chain overshoots the small sprocket. Turn anti-clockwise if the chain won't go into it.

Turn low adjustment screw* clockwise if the chain overshoots the large sprocket. Turn anti-clockwise if the chain won't go into it.

Front derailleur

Turn inside limit screw** clockwise if the chain overshoots the small chainwheel. Turn it anti-clockwise if it won't go into the small chainwheel.

Turn outside limit screw** clockwise if the chain overshoots the large chainwheel. Turn it anti-clockwise if it won't go into the large chainwheel.

 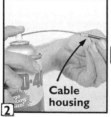  

1 Put the chain on the smallest cog and chainwheel. Notice the route the cable takes. Loosen the cable anchor bolt, pull the gear lever and release it a few times. Pull out the cable wire with pliers.

2 Spray lubricant in the housings, or if they are split, replace them. Now, remembering where the old cable went, thread new cable through the gear lever, cable housing and bottom bracket guide.

3 Thread the new cable through the rear derailleur housing, then through the cable anchor bolt. Pull it tightly by hand or with pliers, then tighten the anchor bolt using a spanner or allen key.

4 Trim off any extra cable. Put a cap on the end of the cable to stop it fraying. Try out the gears to make sure the cable is secure. Finally, retighten the cable if it goes slack; new cable often stretches.

*Most rear derailleurs have an H and an L to mark the high and low screw.
**The inside screw is the one closest to the frame.

If you want to ride your bike with confidence, you must be certain that your brakes will not fail you when you need them. Never go out on your bike without checking your brakes (see page 6). The steps on these two pages will enable you to overhaul them.

How they work

There is a cable running from each brake lever to the two brake units. Different bikes have different types of brake unit, but most mountain bikes have the tough cantilever brakes shown in the picture below.

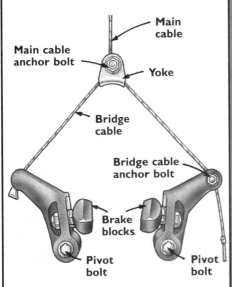

Main cable

Main cable anchor bolt

Yoke

Bridge cable

Bridge cable anchor bolt

Brake blocks

Pivot bolt

Pivot bolt

The main brake cable is secured to the yoke of the brake unit by a cable anchor bolt. In addition to this, a cable (called a bridge cable or straddle wire) loops through the yoke.

When you pull on the brake lever, the yoke pulls on the brake unit. The unit then pivots, pushing the blocks against the rim of the wheel.

Tensioning the brakes

If the brakes take a long time to respond, or they are rubbing against the rim as you ride, it could be because the brake tension is wrong. To adjust the tension, you will need to ask a friend to help you.

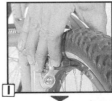

1 Ask your friend to squeeze the brake blocks as firmly as possible against the rim of the wheel.

2 Loosen the cable anchor bolt. Pull some cable through or release some, then retighten the bolt.

3 Ask your friend to let go. Pull on the brake levers a few times to check the tension.

Bridge cable tension

Your bike may have a bridge cable anchor bolt which allows you to alter the tension here instead.

4 Ask your friend to hold the brake blocks against the rim. Undo the bridge cable anchor bolt.

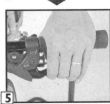

5 Release some bridge cable, or pull some through. Retighten the nut and test the brakes as above.

*You may also need to readjust the brake blocks as shown above.

Adjusting the brake blocks

It is important that the whole of each brake block hits the rim. If it is too high, it will damage the tyre. If it is too low, it will lose braking power.

To stop it from squeaking, angle it so that the front part hits the rim first. This is called "toeing the brake in".

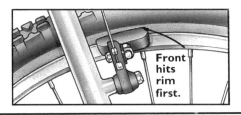

Front hits rim first.

To adjust a brake block, loosen the brake block nut and move the block. Retighten the nut securely.

Replacing a brake block

Worn brake blocks don't work effectively. Replacing them is cheap and easy.

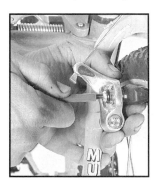

Loosen the brake block nut and ease out the old block. Replace with a new one, positioning it correctly (see above) before tightening the nut.

Replacing a worn brake cable

A worn brake cable is likely to snap when you put a lot of stress on it. For obvious reasons, this is something you want to avoid. Replace brake cables as soon as they start to fray or rust.

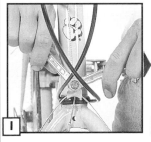

1

Notice the route the cable takes between the anchor bolt and the brake lever. Release one end from the bolt and the other from the lever. Remove from housing.

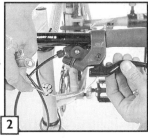

2

Spray lubricant inside the housing, or replace it if it is cracked. Install a new cable into the brake lever. Pull firmly on the cable and lever to ensure the cable is secure.

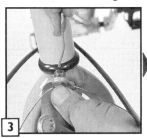

3

Thread the cable into the housing. Remembering the route of the old cable, position the new cable through all the guides along the frame towards the anchor bolt.

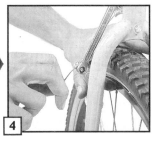

4

Slip the cable through the anchor bolt, then loop the bridge cable over the yoke. Finally, adjust the brakes by tensioning the brake or bridge cable as described above.

Maintenance 4: Wheels and hubs

Do you live in horror of getting a problem in your back wheel, such as a puncture or broken spoke? If so, this is probably because you don't know how to remove or replace the back wheel or freewheel. The following steps will show you how to do this.

How it works

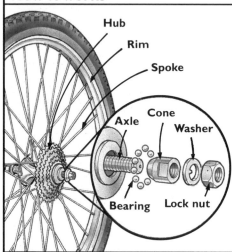

Hub
Rim
Spoke
Axle
Cone
Washer
Bearing
Lock nut

The wheel is made up of a hub and rim, held together by spokes. The spokes must be tensioned correctly for the wheel to rotate evenly. This is a specialist job; have your wheels retensioned by a mechanic if they are buckled.

The hub consists of an axle, a cone, bearings, washers and a lock nut. The bearings allow the wheel to turn while the axle stays still. The axle is fixed in the frame by means of axle nut or a quick-release (QR).

On the back wheel, there is a freewheel. This enables the wheel to rotate forwards without turning the rear sprockets and the pedals with it. This means that you can coast along the road without the pedals turning.

Checking the bearings

Sometimes the hub bearings get so full of dirt and grit that they don't work properly. Alternatively, they may become worn and too loose. Check yours as described on the right. If you do find a problem, replace the bearings (see below).

Too tight?

Remove the wheel, and hold it by the axle. Now spin it. It should turn without resistance from the hub.

Too loose?

Hold the wheel by the axle, and rock it from side to side. There should be no sideways movement in the hub.*

Overhauling the hub

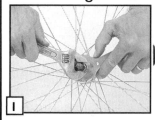

1

Holding the hub cone with a cone spanner, use an adjustable spanner to take off the lock nut.

2

Remove the washers, cone and bearings. Remove the axle from the other side of the hub.

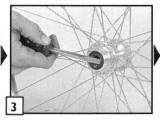

3

Use a wide screwdriver to take out the dust covers gently. Now clean the cone, axle and hub.

*On a QR system, there can be a little movement.

Removing the back wheel

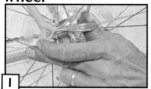

1

With chain in the small sprocket, pull short end of bridge cable to open brake. Open QR or axle nuts.

2

Push the wheel forwards and pull the rear derailleur hanger back, as shown in the photo above.*

3

Lift the back of the bike until the wheel falls clear of the chain. Remove the wheel.

Replacing the back wheel

1

Holding the chain with your right hand, position the wheel inside the frame.*

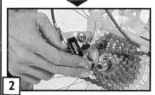

2

Now carefully position the chain on to the teeth of the smallest cog in the freewheel.

3

Slide the axle into the drop-outs, ensuring the wheel is centred. Tighten the QR or axle nuts.

Removing the freewheel

1

Remove the wheel. Put the freewheel remover in the freewheel. Secure it with the QR or axle nut.

2

Put a spanner over the freewheel remover as shown above, then push on it with all your weight.

3

When the freewheel gives, undo the QR or nut and unscrew the freewheel with the remover.**

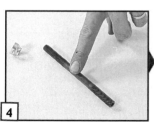

4

Inspect the cone for pitting. Roll the axle; it will move unevenly if bent. Replace if necessary.

5

Use your fingers to put grease in the hub. Now install the new bearings inside the hub.

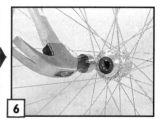

6

Gently tap in the dust covers with a hammer. Reassemble the other parts in reverse order.

*If you don't have a bike stand, you might need someone to hold the bike.
**When you put it back, screw it on firmly by hand. It will tighten itself when you ride.

Maintenance 5: Bottom bracket

Because the bottom bracket is so close to the ground it is an obvious target for any grit, mud, water and so on that is thrown off the front wheel while you are riding. For this reason, it is important that you overhaul it regularly. This is called "repacking the bottom bracket".

How it works

The bottom bracket is really the heart of the bicycle. It contains an axle, fixed in place by two bearings. The two cranks revolve around these bearings when you pedal.

At one end of the axle there is a fixed cup. At the other end is an adjustable cup which allows you to tighten or loosen the movement of the axle. The adjustable cup is held in place by a lock ring.

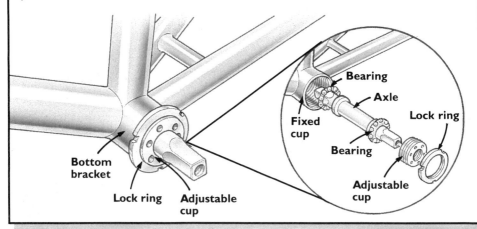

Bottom bracket

Lock ring   Adjustable cup

Bearing

Axle

Lock ring

Fixed cup

Bearing

Adjustable cup

Checking the axle movement

The test on the right will enable you to see whether the axle is too tight or too loose. Generally, you can correct the movement by adjusting the bearings (see far right). Although the photo shows this with the cranks off, you can do it with them on.

You may find that you cannot make the axle any tighter, or make it run smoothly. If so, the bearings are badly worn, and you should replace them when repacking the bottom bracket.

Testing for loose bearings.

A. Hold each crank by the pedal and rock it. If there is play at the axle, the bearings are too loose.
B. Rest the front of the chain on the bottom bracket and spin the cranks. If you feel resistance, the bearings are too tight.

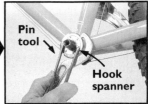

Pin tool

Hook spanner

To adjust the bearings, undo the lock ring and hold it steady with a hook spanner. To make the bearings tighter, screw in the adjustable cup with a pin tool. To loosen, undo the cup slightly. Retighten the lock ring while holding the cup steady.

Removing the cranks

In order to repack the bottom bracket, you need first to remove the cranks.

Pin tool

1

Put the chain on the large chainwheel.* Remove the dust caps. Now, using the crank spanner, remove each nut or bolt and washer.

2

Firmly screw the crank removing tool into one of the cranks. Turn the outside bolt on the tool, holding on to the pedal for leverage.

3

Remove the crank to expose the cup and spindle. Now remove the other crank. Clean the bottom bracket with a rag and spray lubricant.

Repacking the bottom bracket

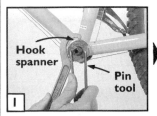

Hook spanner

Pin tool

1

Remove the cranks. Now remove the lock ring on the left side.

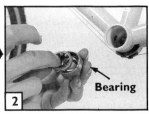

Bearing

2

Carefully remove the adjustable cup with a pin tool. Take out the bearing.

Adjustable cup

3

Clean the cup with lubricant, then inspect it. If it's pitted, renew it.

Axle

4

Remove the axle. Now spray it with lubricant and clean it thoroughly.

Dust shield

5

If your bike has a dust shield in the bottom bracket shell, remove it.

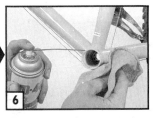

6

Remove the bearing and fixed cup.** Clean the cup and bottom bracket shell.

7

Reassemble the axle parts in reverse order, liberally greasing them.

8

Tap the cranks on with a hammer. Screw in nuts, then tighten with spanner.

*This stops the teeth cutting your hand if the spanner slips.
**On most bikes, you turn the fixed cup clockwise to remove it.

Maintenance 6: Headset

Most steering problems occur because the headset is worn or dirty, or too tight or loose. Follow these steps to overhaul yours.

How it works

The headset is the centre of the steering system. It consists of a set of bearings at each end of the head tube. When you turn the handlebars, the headset bearings turn too, enabling the front fork and wheel to move with them.

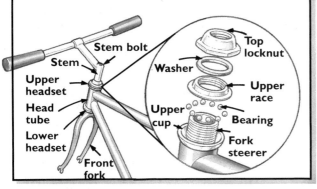

Checking the headset movement

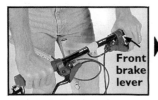

Front brake lever

Hold wheel between legs

Hold the front brake lever tightly and rock the bike backwards and forwards. There should be no rattling from the front fork or the handlebars.

Problems?

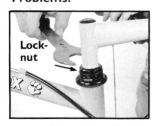

Lock-nut

Pick up the front of the bike and turn the handlebars left and right as far as they will go. They should turn without resistance or binding.

Undo the top locknut. Tighten or loosen the upper race. Retighten the locknut.

Carry out the tests again and adjust the upper race until it is neither too tight nor too loose.

The overhaul

Stem bolt

1

Loosen the stem bolt with a spanner or allen key. Tap the bolt with a plastic hammer or block of wood if necessary.

5

Start unscrewing the upper race. This holds the fork in the frame, so you will have to support the fork from below.

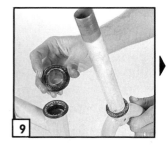

9

Replace the bearing cups and bearings on the fork and headtube. Now fit the front fork back into the frame.

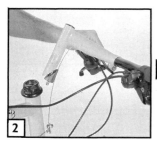

2 Remove the handlebars from the frame (you may have to pull hard). Use a rag to clean any grease and rust from the stem.

3 Allow the handlebars to hang gently to one side of the frame. Make sure they do not bump or scratch the frame.

4 Remove the top locknut from the frame, using a spanner. Now remove any washers or reflector brackets.

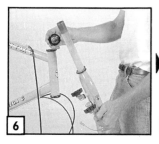

6 Making sure no bearings fall out, remove the upper race from the head tube. Now remove the fork from the frame.

7 Clean all parts including the fork and inside the frame. Look at the races; if they're worn or pitted, renew the headset.

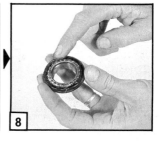

8 Next, rub a generous amount of new grease into the bearing cups and bearings with the tips of your fingers.

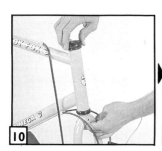

10 Screw the upper race on to the head tube until it is just hand-tight. Put the washers and brackets back in the right order.

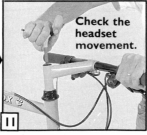

Check the headset movement.

11 Holding the upper race with a spanner, replace the lock nut. Fit the handlebars at the correct height (see right).

Handlebar height

The handlebars can be positioned anywhere between the height of the saddle and 5cm (2 ins) below it, depending on which you find most comfortable.

Always keep at least 5cm of stem in the head tube to ensure it doesn't break. If 5cm line isn't marked, do it yourself with an indelible pen.

Going further

Joining a mountain bike organization is a very good way to get the best out of the sport. Many provide you with information on competitions, routes, books and so on. Some fight on your behalf to keep tracks open to cyclists and improve the image of mountain bike riding as a sport. Nearly all of them support local clubs and put you in touch with enthusiasts in your area.

Great Britain

The Mountain Bike Club
1 Santon House
Santon
Downham
Suffolk IP7 OTT
GB

The British Cyclo-Cross Association
59 Jordan Road
Sutton Coldfield
West Midlands, B75 5AE
GB

USA

Bikecentennial
PO Box 8308
Missoula, MT 59807
USA

LAW (League of American Wheelmen)
Suite 209
6707 Whitestone Road
Baltimore, MD 21207
USA

NORBA (National Off-Road Bicycling Association)
1750 E. Boulder
Colorado Springs
CO 80909
USA

Canada

Canadian Cycling Association
1600 prom. James Naismith Drive
Gloucester
Ontario
Canada KIB 5N4

Ontario Cycling Association
1220 Sheppard Ave. E.
Willowdale
Ontario
Canada M2K 2XI

WORCA (Whistler Off-Road Cycling Association)
Box 796
Whistler, B.C.
Canada VON 180

Australia

Australian Mountain Bike Association
P.O. Box N25
Grosvenor Place
Sydney, NSW 2000
Australia

New Zealand

New Zealand Mountain Bike Association
PO Box 388 Waikato Mail Centre
Hamilton
New Zealand

International

International Mountain Bike Association
Route 2, Box 303
Bishop, CA 93514
USA

Glossary

Adjustable cup A threaded **bearing cup** which controls the adjustment of the bottom bracket bearings.

Allen key A six-sided, L-shaped tool used on certain bolts.

Axle A rod around which the cranks or hubs rotate.

Bearing cup A cylindrical holder which contains steel balls and grease. The **axle** rotates on the steel balls.

Binder bolt Bolt which holds the seatpost in place.

Brake blocks The rubber blocks in the brake that rub against the rim when the brake is on.

Chain tool A tool for breaking apart or rejoining a chain. It does this by pushing a pin in or out.

Cone spanner A spanner that is very thin so it can fit hub cones.

Cotterless crank removing tool A device that screws into a crank and pulls it off the axle.

Crank spanner A spanner that tightens the bolt or nut which holds the crank on to the bottom bracket **axle.**

Drop-outs The slots on the frame inside which the front and back wheel are clamped.

Dust cap A threaded cover that screws into the crank. It protects the bolt and washer that hold the crank on the **axle.** It also protects the threads which the **cotterless crank removing tool** screws into.

Dust shield A cover that keeps dust out of the bearings.

Fixed cup A threaded **bearing cup** which holds the bottom bracket **axle** and bearings on the chainwheel side.

Freewheel remover A tool that fits into the freewheel and, with the aid of a spanner, removes the freewheel from the hub.

Hook spanner A spanner used to loosen or tighten the **lock ring** on the bottom bracket bearings.

Inner tube Rubber tube which fits inside a tyre and holds the air when you pump it up.

Lock ring A threaded ring which screws on to the **adjustable cup** and prevents it from coming loose.

Pin tool A tool with two pins on a Y-shaped spanner used for turning the **adjustable cup** on the bottom bracket.

Pressure gauge A device that measures the air pressure in the tyre when you press it on to the tyre **valve.**

psi Pounds per square inch. Unit of measurement used to indicate the amount of air pressure in a tyre. The metric measurement is atmospheres, but most manufacturers usually use the non-metric psi units.

Race A circular metal ring that is used as a track for ball bearings to roll on.

Spoke nipple tool A small hand-held spanner that fits on to the spoke nipple. It is used to increase or decrease spoke tension between the rim and hub.

Tyre lever A plastic or metal lever used to remove the tyre from the rim.

Valve The device on an **inner tube** through which air is pumped or released.

The future of mountain bikes

Manufacturers and enthusiasts alike are constantly trying to improve the strength, speed and comfort of mountain bikes. It is a very exciting time for anyone keen to improve the performance of his or her bike.

Here are some of the ideas that designers are currently working on.

One-piece frames

Most frames consist of several tubes joined together. Unfortunately, the joints tend to get an enormous amount of stress. Some designers are now building one-piece frames made of carbon-fibre, which don't need any joints. These are being produced on a small scale because the technology is very new, and mass production techniques have not yet been devised.

Suspension

Another problem that designers are trying to overcome is the lack of control you experience when you hit bumps. They are creating suspension systems to deal with this. Many of these have problems of their own. Firstly, they absorb your pedalling energy. Secondly, they alter the geometry of a bike, making certain manoeuvres hazardous. Finally, they can be very heavy.

There are now two designs which solve all these problems. So suspension systems may become standard fixtures on mountain bikes before too long.

Twisting gear levers

The most recent development in gear levers is the twist-grip shifter. This is like a normal handlebar grip, but as you swivel it round, it changes gear. This means there is no need to take your hands off the handlebars at all.

A future innovation may be to change gear by pressing a button, thus sending an electronic impulse to the gears via the cables.

Saddles and handlebars

Most improvements have been for racing; a more stretched-out riding position, and lighter, firmer saddles. But most off-road riders need a bike that will help them when the terrain gets rough. Here, it is better to have handlebars closer to the body for balance, and softer saddles. Soon there may be two types of mountain bike; one for racing, and one for off-road stunts.

Hidden gears

Before the derailleur system, gears were enclosed inside the hubs. Although these are now considered old-fashioned, they do have advantages. For example, as the whole gear system is enclosed in the hub, it is unaffected by mud and so on. Also, it requires very little maintenance.

There are disadvantages with the hub systems currently available. In particular, they provide only a limited range of gears, and are too weak for off-road use. However, these problems could be overcome, and the hub system may well make a comeback in future years.

Buying new parts

There are lots of new components (such as lights, toe-clips and tools) coming on the market every month. Some work well; others are just gimmicks. Before you buy anything, look at cycling magazines. These often have valuable buyers' guides.

If you do buy something which turns out to be a dud, put it down to experience.

RACING BIKES

Jessica Kent

Edited by **Judy Tatchell**

Consultants: **Patrick Field**
and **Tricia Liggett**

Designed by **Richard Johnson**

Additional designs by **John Beaumont**

Cover design by **Stephen Wright**

Illustrated by **Kim Raymond**
and **Kuo Kang Chen**

Colour photography by **David Cannon, Allsport UK**
Black and white photography by **Jane Munro Photography**

Models: **Stuart** and **Rachel McGee, Colin Clarke**
and **Catherine Harthill**

This book was produced in association with  *Falcon*

Contents

Using part two

To be a successful racing cyclist, you need a combination of good technique and tactical skill. This book can help you develop the style, strategies and mental approaches that will help you win different types of race.

In a road race you have to conserve your energy so that you can make your main efforts at strategic moments.

For some track races, you need to be a wily tactician. Others rely solely on speed and determination.

You have to do without other riders spurring you on when you race against the clock in a time trial.

You face many different situations and obstacles in cyclo-cross which require special techniques.

Training

Consistent training is a must. This book tells you how to get yourself in condition by following a training programme of exercise both on and off the bike.

Joining a club

Joining a local cycle club can benefit you, too. You get coaching and it is easier and more fun to train with other people. You need to belong to a club to enter most races.

Bike technology

There are certain design features unique to racing bikes. In this book, you can find out about bike technology and how performance can be improved.

Some early champions

The first cycle race was held in Paris on 31 May 1868. It was won by an Englishman, James Moore. He rode an early type of bicycle called a velocipede, like the one on the right.

Major Taylor from Indiana overcame racial prejudice to become a world class sprinter at 16, a professional at 18 and a world champion at 20.

Melle Lisette (Amélie le Gall), a French cyclist, won the first official Women's World Championship in 1896.

About racing bikes

How fast a racing bike can go depends on its design and how light it is as well as on your skill as a rider.

Here are some of the special features of a standard racing bike.

Frame

Racing frames are made of lightweight alloy steel tubing. Professional machines may be made of aluminium or carbon fibre which are even lighter and much more expensive.

The forks are straighter than on an ordinary bike to make the steering more responsive. The chainstays are short, making the bike more rigid and efficient. These leave no room for mudguards.

Toeclips

Toeclips help you to exert pressure on the pedal all the way round: you can pull up as well as push down. An alternative design of pedal, called a system pedal, fixes your shoe to the pedal. (There is more about these on page 90.)

Handlebars

Dropped handlebars let you crouch low and keep a streamlined shape.

Saddle

A racing saddle is very narrow at the front. This reduces rubbing on the inside of your thighs.

Brakes

Racing bikes have side-pull brakes which allow you to brake slowly or hard.

Cable

Caliper

Brake shoe

As you brake, the cable is pulled up. This draws the arms (calipers) together and the rim is squeezed between the brake blocks.

Hubs

Racing hubs have quick-release levers so that you can change a wheel in seconds if you have a puncture.

Top tube

Head tube

Rear sprockets and derailleur (see opposite).

Down tube

Seat tube

Water bottle and cage for long rides.

Seat stay

Forks

Quick-release lever

Crank

Chainset (see opposite)

Chainstay

Wheels and tyres

Narrow wheel rims and tyres reduce contact with the road. This cuts down on friction between the tyres and the road (called rolling resistance) so the bike can go faster. Good rims and hubs are made of light aluminium alloy.

High-pressure, or wired-on, tyres have a removable inner tube. You repair a puncture by patching the inner tube.

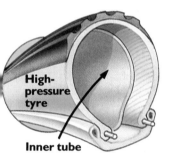

High-pressure tyre

Inner tube

Tubular tyres (tubs) have sewn-in tubes. The tyre is glued on to the rim. Tubs are lighter than high-pressure tyres but if you get a puncture they need specialist repair, making them expensive to use.

The alloy rims used with tubs are called sprints. You cannot use sprints with high-pressure tyres.

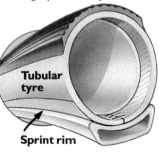

Tubular tyre

Sprint rim

Gears

Most racing bikes have ten or twelve gears. These help you to maintain an efficient pedalling rate, or cadence, on different surfaces and gradients.

Sprockets and chainwheels are described by the number of teeth they have. The set of five or six rear sprockets and freewheel mechanism is called a block.

Chain is shifted by derailleur and front changer (not shown).

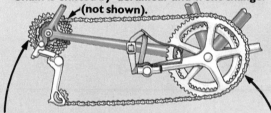

A racing block might have sprockets with 13, 14, 15, 16, 17 and 18 teeth.

A racing chainset might have two chainwheels with 52 and 42 teeth.

How gears work

As you pedal, the distance the wheels travel is determined by the gear you are in. One turn of the pedals in a low gear will not take you as far as it will in a higher gear. A lower gear enables you to apply more pressure over a certain distance, for instance when you are going uphill or accelerating.

In the highest gear, the chain sits on the bigger chainwheel and the smallest sprocket.

Each time the pedals turn, the wheel goes round nearly four times.

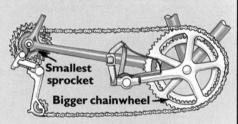

Smallest sprocket

Bigger chainwheel

In the lowest gear, the chain sits on the smaller chainwheel and the biggest sprocket.

Each time the pedals turn, the wheel goes round just over twice.

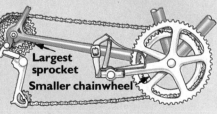

Largest sprocket

Smaller chainwheel

Getting started

You don't need much specialist gear for cycle training but there are rules about what you can wear to enter some races. Also, certain items of clothing and equipment can make cycling more comfortable, efficient and safe. Some of these are shown below.

What to wear

The gear shown here is specially designed for cycling.* However, to start with you can wear shorts or a track suit for training, with a pair of trainers.

Cycling shoes have stiff soles so that all your pedalling power is transmitted to the pedal. The force is distributed over the whole foot so your feet do not get so tired.

You can fit shoe-plates, or cleats, to the soles to keep the shoe in position on the pedal.

You should always protect your head with a helmet, whether training or racing. Helmets are often compulsory in races. You can find out more about different kinds of helmet on page 77.

Skin-tight shorts and shirts offer less wind-resistance than baggy clothes.

Keeping warm

You get tired more quickly when you are cold. Thermal clothing is efficient but expensive. Instead, try wearing several thin, close-fitting layers under a cycling jersey. You can even put a few sheets of newspaper or a polythene bag up the front of your jersey to keep a cold wind off your chest.

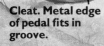

Cleat. Metal edge of pedal fits in groove.

Gloves

As well as being warm, gloves absorb vibrations from the road. They also protect your palms in a fall when your hands often hit the road first.

Adjust the cleats so that your feet sit straight on the pedals. Otherwise you might damage your knees.

Walking around in cycling shoes reduces their stiffness and wears out the cleats so don't do it more than you have to.

Be seen!

Bright clothes and fluorescent strips can save your life by warning motorists of your presence on the road.

There is more about specialist clothing and equipment on pages 76-77 and 86-87.

Equipment and tools

You should be prepared to carry out minor repairs on any ride. Take a basic set of tools and equipment with you, such as the one shown on the right.

Put the tools in an old sock or roll them up in a rag and tie them under the saddle.

When you are out with a group, you only need one set of tools between you. Take your own spare inner tube, though.

Lights increase the chances of you being seen in the rain as well as in the dark.

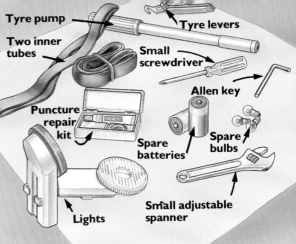

Tyre pump

Tyre levers

Two inner tubes

Small screwdriver

Allen key

Puncture repair kit

Spare batteries

Spare bulbs

Lights

Small adjustable spanner

Setting up your bike

Check that your saddle and handlebars are adjusted to suit your height.* This helps you to use your leg, arm and back muscles efficiently as you ride.

Saddle height

Seat post

Ask a friend to hold your bike. Sit with your hips level. With the crank at its lowest point and your foot flat on the pedal, your leg should be nearly straight.

With the cranks horizontal, your front knee should be directly over your toe. This is not easy to see for yourself so ask a friend to check for you. Move the saddle forwards or back until it is right.

The top of the saddle should be horizontal.

There should be at least 5cm of the seat post inside the seat tube for safety.

Handlebars

You need to feel comfortable in these three positions.

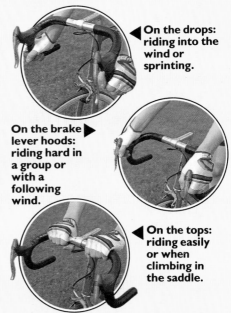

On the drops: riding into the wind or sprinting.

On the brake lever hoods: riding hard in a group or with a following wind.

On the tops: riding easily or when climbing in the saddle.

To start with, set your bars about level with your saddle. As your back gets stronger, you can lower them for a more streamlined position. As a rough guide, the bars should prevent you from seeing the front hub when you are on the drops.

*You can find out how to make these adjustments on page 84.

55

Riding techniques

The techniques on this page are all quite basic but you need to be able to do them automatically and with confidence. Then you will be free to concentrate on the tactics which will help you to win a race.

Ankling

Ankling technique increases the force you exert on the pedal. You use the toeclip to pull up as well as push down on it.

Pushing down.

Pulling up.

People develop different styles but the picture shows how your ankle might bend as you push down, pull back, pull up and push the pedal forwards over the top.

Ankling is more effective at low cadences, for instance when you are climbing.

A cleat enables you to pull up and back on the pedal when your foot is pointing downwards, without your foot slipping out of the toeclip.

Pedalling rate: cadence

In general, a fairly brisk cadence is the most efficient: you can keep a steady pressure on the pedals without getting too tired. When training, aim for a minimum average of between 75 and 100 pedal revolutions per minute, or rpm. (To find your rpm, count the revolutions in ten seconds and multiply by six.) Use your gears to maintain the cadence. Also, practise pedalling at a rate of 100 – 150 rpm for a few minutes at a time. This is good sprint practice.

Changing gear

To change gear smoothly without losing too much speed, keep pedalling but take the pressure off the pedals as you gently move the gear levers.

Limit your use of the inside chainwheel and the outside sprocket and vice versa. The steep angle of the chain slightly increases the friction between it and the chainwheel and sprocket.

If the chain comes off, ease off on the pedals. Try coaxing it back on by pedalling very lightly and gently moving the gear levers. You may be able to lean down and lift it back on to a chainwheel with your fingers. If these remedies do not work, don't risk jamming it: dismount and replace it by hand.

Practice tip

Ankling with one leg at a time is very good practice. Take one foot right out of its toeclip and make sure the other toestrap is tight.

Hold your free foot out of the way.

Try to keep an even pressure on the pedal

all the way round. Then change legs.

Reaching speed

Don't start in too low a gear or you will waste energy pedalling furiously and not getting very far. Try starting on the big chainwheel, one or two sprockets below the one you use for cruising. Or start on your cruising sprocket but on the little wheel. Then you just need to shift to the big one when your cadence has increased.

Climbing

Change down just before you reach a hill. If you leave it until half way up, you lose speed and may stall completely on a steep hill.

Stay in the saddle in your lowest gear for as long as you can. If you need more power, stand up on the pedals and use your weight to push down. This is called honking. Keep your weight back so that your back wheel does not slip.

Braking

★ Try to look ahead and avoid problems by slowing down gently rather than braking suddenly and losing more speed than necessary.

★ If you have to brake suddenly when riding fast, put both brakes on hard and then ease off the pressure as the bike slows down, to avoid skidding.

★ Use both brakes evenly. Too much pressure on the front brake may make the back wheel lift off. Braking too hard with the back brake can make the wheel skid.

★ Shift your body weight back and down as you brake to help stabilize the bike.

★ In the wet, your brakes may lose their grip on the slippery wheel rims. Brake rapidly on and off to clear water off them so the brakes can grip properly.

Cornering at speed

If you must brake to get round a corner, do so as you approach it and not as you go round. Change down in advance so that you can accelerate out of the corner. Keep your weight back for stability.

The faster you go, the more you lean into the corner. Stop pedalling and make sure your inside pedal is up or it might catch the ground and you will fall off.

On sharp corners, hold your inside knee away from your body to act as a counter-weight.

You corner faster at the front in a race. Near the back, you have to brake earlier as the leaders slow down for the bend. By the time you reach it, they are speeding off ahead, leaving a gap for you to close.

To keep your speed up, try to smooth the bend off by swinging out slightly as you enter it. Look behind before you do this and NEVER cross into the opposite lane.

Bike-handling

The faster you go on your bike, the quicker your reactions need to be. You have to be able to take immediate avoiding action when suddenly confronted with a deep pothole, a car door opening in your path or even a fallen cyclist. The following techniques can help you tackle such hazards.

Practise these techniques where there are no other vehicles and where you will have a soft landing if you fall.

Avoiding obstacles

Here is a quick way to whip round an obstacle in your path while barely losing speed. To start with, don't practise with an obstacle that might damage you or your bike if you crash.

Reduce speed very slightly as you approach the obstacle.

Just before you reach it, flick your handlebars towards it. This makes the bike lean away from the obstacle.

As the bike leans away from the obstacle, steer away from it. The lean helps you to make a very sharp turn round it.

Correct your course to continue.

Jumping the bike

If you don't have room to steer round an obstacle or pothole, you may need to jump over it. Practise this without an obstacle first. Then try jumping something low that will not damage the wheels if you land on it.

Accelerate hard. Then freewheel for a moment as you throw your weight back and pull up on the handlebars to lift the front wheel.

As soon as the front wheel comes up, throw your weight forwards and pull up on the pedals using your toeclips. This lifts the back wheel.

You will find that the faster you are travelling, the further you can jump on the bike.

Practise lifting the back wheel before the front wheel touches the ground. Then see if you can do the whole jump in one movement: lift your body sharply, then bend your arms and legs to bring the bike up with you.

Jumping sideways

You can combine the previous two techniques to jump across a ridge or a rut in a road or track. Try practising with a chalk line to represent a ridge.

Steer sharply away from the ridge to make the bike lean towards it. As soon as this happens, steer towards it.

As you steer towards the ridge, pull up sharply on the handlebars to lift the front wheel up over it.

As the front wheel lifts off the ground, lean forwards and pull up on the toeclips to lift the back wheel.

As you get better at doing this, you should find that you can lift both wheels off the ground at the same time.

Dips and potholes

Crashing through dips and potholes puts strain on both you and your bike. Shift your weight as shown to reduce this.

| Into a dip. | Weight back, off saddle. | Pull up on bars. |
| Out of a dip. | Weight over front wheel. | Pull up on rear wheel. |

Rough roads

On bumpy surfaces, keep your weight just off the saddle and bend your arms a bit. Your bent limbs act as shock absorbers.

Supporting your weight on the pedals keeps the centre of gravity low. It may be easier to use a higher gear than normal.

Practice tips

★ Don't practise the jumping and avoidance techniques on the open road until you are sure you have mastered them.

★ Wear a thick tracksuit, gloves and a helmet to protect yourself.

★ If you fall, protect your head by folding your arms around it. You can find out more about falling on page 89.

★ Try to stay relaxed even in awkward situations. If you tense up, you will ride erratically.

Time trials

A time trial is a flat-out race against the clock over a fixed distance. Most take place on the open road but there are also time trials on cycle tracks. Because they are timed, they can help you to measure your own improvement.

Time trials for under-16s are usually between 10 and 40km long. Senior races can be up to 160km. Competitors start at one-minute intervals and follow a marked route, with marshals to direct you at road junctions.

Before the race

Time trials are extremely demanding so you need to warm your muscles up before you start. (In general, the shorter an event, the longer the warm up, because the start will be more violent.) A good way to warm up is to ride to the start if it is not more than an hour's gentle ride away. Then do some stretches such as those on pages 72-73.

Practice tip

At the start of a race you need a helper to hold your bike up as shown. Ask someone to practise this with you. They can either hold the lip of the saddle at the back or stand next to you, holding the seat post and handlebars.

Start with the cranks about 11 o'clock and 5 o'clock. Try to get a powerful start with no wobbling.

The time trial bike

You can ride a time trial on any racing bike but keep it as light as you can. If you can afford them, you can buy special time trial wheels which have fewer spokes to cut down on weight.

As most courses are fairly flat, you can remove a chainwheel: five or six close-ratio gears* are enough. The block should allow you to keep your feet spinning at 100rpm at least.

*Each sprocket on a close-ratio block has one more tooth than the last. This gives you a lot of choice within a fairly small range.

During the race

Keep your focus on the road ahead. Don't look back or you will lose concentration and speed.

Maintain a steady cadence throughout. Counting your pedal revolutions can help you strike up a rhythm.

Maintain your effort just below the point at which you become exhausted. If you go over this limit, you will waste time slowing down to recover.

Race tip

As you don't have many gears, you may have to rise out of the saddle to keep your cadence up on hills.

Team time trials

In a team time trial, teams of two or four riders compete over a course of up to 100km. Members of the team take turns at the front to keep the pace up.* The time registered is that of the second person of a team of two or the third of a team of four.

Technique tip

Keep your body low, your elbows tucked in and your head still for minimum aerodynamic drag.

Race food

In an event of 40km or more, you will need water. Over 75km you will also need food or an energy drink to keep up your energy reserves.**

You can carry small snacks in the pockets of your jersey. Undo packets in advance so the food is easy to get at with one hand. Peel fruit and wrap in foil for easy access.

Start drinking after about 15 minutes. Don't wait until you are thirsty. Eating and drinking little and often saves your body from having to work hard at digestion.

Eat or drink when you are riding on the flat and in a straight line: climbing, descending and cornering demand your full concentration.

Water is heavy so experiment on training runs to find out how much you need. Don't forget you will need more on hot days.

*See page 63 for more about riding in a group.
**See page 91 for more about food and energy drinks.

Road racing

In a road race, you race against other riders, not the clock. This calls for different tactics.

Most road races are massed start events, where all the riders start together. These are called scratch races. In others, called handicap races, some categories of entrant such as Juniors (see right) may be given a head start.

Categories

Professionals . . paid team members
Firsts . . . . top class amateurs
Seconds . . second class amateurs
Thirds . . . . . . other riders over 18
Juniors . . . . 16-18 year olds
Juveniles. . . . . under 16
Veterans . . . . over 40

Closed-circuit races

Some races are held on routes closed to traffic in town centres, parks or industrial estates. These are called criteriums. All Juvenile races are held on closed circuits because Juveniles are not allowed to race on the open road.

In a race on the open road, a car with a warning sign travels in front and marshals stand along the route. You have to obey all the rules of the road.

Race distances

Juvenile races are usually 16 or 40km long. Junior races vary between 40 and 100km. More senior races are usually 100-120km but may be up to 200km long.

You score points for doing well in a race and move up a category when you have scored the necessary number of points.

Before the race

Before the race, your bike will be checked by officials to make sure it is roadworthy.

Try to position yourself somewhere near the front in a massed start to avoid being delayed by slow starters. This is particularly important in criteriums which tend to start very fast.

Practice tip

Practise pushing off and getting your free foot into the toeclip before the crank has completed one revolution. This is better than trying to get your foot in and speed up at the same time.

Riding in a bunch

By tucking in close behind another rider, you can travel as fast as him or her with 15-20% less effort. This is called slipstreaming or wheel-following. A group, or bunch, can travel faster for longer than a lone rider by taking turns at the front. This is called doing bit and bit.

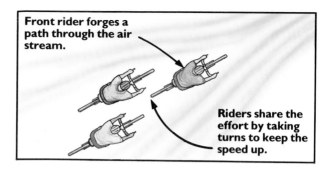

Front rider forges a path through the air stream.

Riders share the effort by taking turns to keep the speed up.

During the race

During the race, the field splits up as smaller groups make an effort to pull away from the main group. This is called making a break or attacking.

Tactics for road racing involve riding with a bunch and co-operating by taking turns at the front. In this way the bunch can travel fast while conserving energy.*

Towards the end of a race you need to be in a bunch near the front. There may be a sprint finish between you and other members of the group. If you have enough energy left, you may be able to make a lone break at the end and leave the others behind.

Take care – if your wheel touches the wheel of the rider in front, you will go over the handlebars.

If there is a sidewind, take shelter accordingly. You can find out more about this over the page.

WIND

Race tips

★ Keep your turns at the front short. Make sure everyone shares the work.
★ Stay alert: look past the rider in front so that you can spot hazards ahead.

FINISH

Practice tip

Wheel-following requires concentration and a very steady speed. Practise by leaving a bike's length between you and the bike in front. As you get used to riding at an even pace, you can gradually reduce this to a minimum of 15cm.

*There is more about this and other race tactics on the next two pages.

63

Road race tactics

It often takes more than power and speed to win. Road race tactics are all about saving energy, placing yourself in the bunch correctly, bluffing and knowing when to relax or make a break. You learn from experience so enter races even if you don't have much chance of winning. Use them to observe and experiment with different tactics.

Before a race

If possible, ride the course before the race or study it on a good map. Note the difficult sections such as hills, corners, narrow or winding sections or areas exposed to the wind. These can be good places to make breaks because the general pace tends to slow down. You need to be near the front on these sections so that you can join any breaks that form.

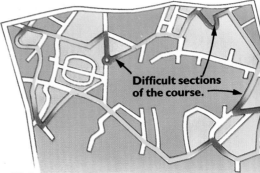

Difficult sections of the course.

Taking shelter

If there is a side wind in a road race, move to the sheltered side of the rider in front. If the road is closed to traffic, the whole bunch can string out across it as shown on the left. This shape is called an *echelon*. If there is traffic on the road, it is not safe to form groups of more than three riders.

You share the effort by taking turns to lead. As a rough guide, turns might last from about 100m to about 500m, depending on the effort needed to keep the pace up. In a small group you need to take longer turns.

Going downhill, a bunch tends to string out for safety and then regroup at the bottom. Going uphill, try to maintain your cadence rather than your speed.

Wind coming from the left.

After a turn, the front rider drops back and joins the end of the bunch.

This rider will then move across to take the lead.

Wind coming from the right. The second rider shelters on the left.

Changing leaders

After a turn at the front, glance back to check the road is clear behind you and to let the other riders know you are about to drop back.

Keep close in as you move back. Accelerate in time to join the back of the bunch or you may drop off the end.

Attacking

In a race, you need to balance energy conservation with riding hard to gain a lead. As you begin an attack, ride hard for about 500m without looking back. Then glance round to see if you have broken away and which riders have followed you.

A bunch is sometimes called a *peloton* (pronouned "pellaton"). This is the French word for it.

In the break

In a break a long way from the finish, it is important to work together to keep the pace up. Only try to split the group up when you feel you have a good chance of getting to the finish alone.

If you need to change up to lead a break, do it before you hit the front so that you can concentrate on maintaining your speed.

Don't attempt to join every break or you will get exhausted. Choose your moments, such as the following:

★ Where other riders are slowing down in difficult sections of the race.
★ Join breaks led by strong riders. These are more likely to succeed.

If you cannot keep up with a break, don't waste energy trying to catch up. Sit up, change down, have a drink, ride steadily and rejoin the bunch.

If you want to overtake, ride up on the sheltered side of the group.

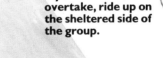

Race tip

Don't attack from the front where your intentions are obvious to everyone. Go from further down the bunch where you can shoot by and surprise the leaders.

Bluffing

If you are feeling the strain of a race, it is likely that others are too. Appearing in control will dishearten them. Ride confidently and try to hide your discomfort. If you then try to attack they may let you go, thinking you are too strong for them.

Mental preparation

A race is a personal thing. Some riders feel they must calm themselves before an event whilst others need to wind themselves up. Don't worry if you cannot sleep the night before a big race. A good night's rest two nights before does you as much good.

Preparing for pain

Push yourself during your training so that you can identify the difference between pain you can ignore and pain that warns of injury. Try not to be put off by physical pain early in a race. Breathe deeply and hang on. Things should soon get easier.

Track racing

Track racing is the fastest form of cycle racing. Both the bikes and the track itself are designed for maximum speed. The ends of the track are steeply banked to help you corner at top speed and the smooth surface cuts down on rolling resistance. Tracks may be indoors or outdoors, with wooden, asphalt or concrete surfaces.

Using the banking

The banked ends of the track help you to stay close to the centre and keep your speed up without slipping as you corner.

You can also use the bank cunningly in races which require tactics as well as speed. It can give you acceleration so that you can swoop down to overtake or intimidate an opponent. Or you can "block" them against the barrier at the top and speed off down the bank in front.

Riding a track bike

A track bike has neither brakes nor gears. There is no freewheel mechanism so you cannot stop pedalling while the bike is in motion. You slow down by restraint on the pedals. This takes some time to get used to, so be careful.

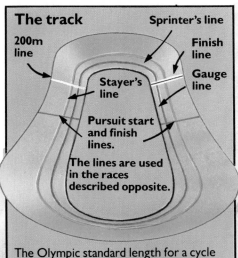

The track

Sprinter's line

200m line

Finish line

Gauge line

Stayer's line

Pursuit start and finish lines.

The lines are used in the races described opposite.

The Olympic standard length for a cycle track is 333.3m but track lengths can vary. A track is measured along the bottom line, or gauge line. You are not allowed to ride below this line.

A bike with no freewheel is called a fixed wheel bike. Lack of brakes or gearing keeps the weight down.

Race tip

The shortest route around the track follows the gauge line. Riding close to this will help you to lap the track quickly.

A short wheelbase makes the bike's steering very responsive.

A high bottom bracket and short cranks allow the pedals clearance on the steep bank.

Having a go

Cycle clubs run "have-a-go" sessions on tracks. They will lend you a bike and give you some coaching. Later on, you can join the track league and take part in the races described below. Remember that track racing is fast and can be dangerous so don't be too ambitious.

Sprint races

In a sprint race, only the last 200m are timed. During the preceding laps, the two riders encourage each other to take the lead so that they can slipstream behind, saving energy for the final sprint.

Tactics are based on bluff and agility. If you are in front, you can try to make your opponent overtake by accelerating and then suddenly slowing down. You can even balance motionless on the track (see below). However, time your tactics carefully so that you are in a position to lead the last 200m.

Track League		RACE POINTS	RUN TOTAL
NAME	CLUB		
T. Ross	Bathby C.C.	6	35
A. Smith	Elmouth C.C.	8	42
S. Leach	Leyton Club	12	28

Practice tip

To practise balancing motionless on the track, keep both pedals horizontal and rock them slightly. Try it where the banking begins at the end of the straight. Turn your handlebars into the bank to help you balance.

Devil take the hindmost

In these races, usually called "devils", the last rider over the line at the end of each lap is withdrawn until only two or three are left. These riders then sprint round the last lap. It is illegal to overtake on the inside of a rider who is inside or on the sprinter's line.

Points races

In a points race, riders compete over a set distance. At the start of some laps, a whistle blows to indicate that these are sprint laps. Points are scored for these by the first three riders to complete them. Double points are scored for the last lap.

Pursuits

In a pursuit race, two riders compete against the clock and each other. They start at opposite sides of the track and try to catch each other up. The rider who closes the gap wins the race. Otherwise the full length course is ridden and whoever covers it in the shortest time is the winner.

Madisons

A Madison is a points race in which up to 20 teams of two people race over a set distance. They take turns to race for a lap each. The person not racing rolls gently around the banking above the stayer's line (see previous page). At the changeover, they are pushed into the race by their partner. Only one rider sprints to the finish line.

To change places, you can use a technique called a handsling. First, you link hands.

Then throw your partner forwards into the race and move back above the stayer's line.

67

Cyclo-cross

Cyclo-cross presents a different set of challenges from other kinds of cycle race. It combines cycling with running and carrying your bike across rough ground and up and down steep hills. You usually get very muddy and wet. You need stamina and agility.

The cyclo-cross season runs through autumn and winter.

The race

Although you may fall off, you shouldn't come to much harm since the race is off-road and the speed tends to be quite slow, with the riders strung out. After a massed start, you have to do as many laps as you can within a set time. Each lap is two or three kilometres long.

The bike and clothing

You can adapt a road bike by changing the gearing and fitting knobbly tyres but a true cyclo-cross bike has a few other differences, as shown below. Most races also allow mountain bikes.

The saddle should be about 5cm lower than on a road bike, for better control.

You can put shoulder pads into your jersey to help you support the bike.

Knobbly tyres grip in the mud.

Wear boots with studded heels for grip and support.

Handlebar gear levers let you change gear without taking your hands off the handlebars.

Cantilever brakes are more powerful than side-pull brakes. They also give more clearance between the brake arms and the wheels so they get less clogged up with mud.

A high bottom bracket gives good ground clearance. A long wheelbase gives the bike more stability.

Gearing that gives you plenty of choice, such as a 13/28 block and 44 chainwheel, helps you cope with different surfaces and gradients. You do not need gears as high as for road races.

Remove anything you don't need from the frame, such as a bottle cage or pump pegs, which may hurt you if you fall off.

Checking the course

★ Arrive early to give yourself time to ride the course before the event.
★ Look out for alternatives to the main path such as routes that avoid really muddy, churned-up ground.
★ Identify the firm ground on steep climbs.
★ Check out obstacles such as tree roots and drainage channels.

Descending

You are likely to encounter steep hills on cyclo-cross courses. You can tackle hills which appear almost vertical from above using the following technique. Practise on short, obstacle-free hills to start with.

Keep your weight back and just off the saddle with your arms almost straight and your pedals level.

Control your speed with the back brake only.

Gates and tree trunks

It is quickest to climb gates and fallen tree trunks with the bike on your shoulder. As you get used to this, you may even be able to vault them. Otherwise swing your bike over and follow unladen.

Getting on and off

You need to be able to get on and off the bike quickly so that you can run with it. Loosen your toeclips so that you can slide your feet out easily.

As you prepare to get off, move your left foot back in the toeclip to help you remove it later. Take your right foot out of the clip.

Press down on the right-hand side of the bars and swing your right leg back over the saddle.

Bring your right leg between your left leg and the frame. Whip your left foot out of the clip and land on your right foot.*

Grab the down tube with your right hand and lift the bike on to your right shoulder.

Loop your right arm round the frame and grasp the lower rung of the left handlebar.

To remount, swing your right leg over the saddle. Don't touch the pedals until your bottom is on the saddle. Then flip the clips over and slide your feet in.

Race tip

Where you can, stay on the bike. It is usually faster to ride than to run with the bike.

Practice tip

Practise dismounting, running and remounting on level ground until you can do it smoothly without losing momentum. You could devise a circuit with trees and so on marking where you get on and off.

*If you are nervous about not getting your foot out in time, bring your right foot round the outside of your left leg instead.

Other cycling events

Other events with something a bit different to offer include cycle speedway, triathlons and hill climbs.

You can find the addresses of the organizations which arrange these races on page 93.

Cycle speedway

Cycle speedway is a fast and furious race that takes place on circuits normally between 50-100m long. The race is usually four laps and lasts about 45 seconds. Four riders compete at a time, either as individuals or as two teams of two.

Speedway technique

The bike has no brakes or gears, so you have to use your feet to slow down on corners.

You need to make a very fast start and aim to lead into the first corner. The skill lies in protecting your lead on subsequent corners.

To prevent a rider sneaking by on the inside, you must stick close to the inside of the track. However, if as a result you swing out as you exit from a corner, an opponent could slip through.

Crash helmets are compulsory for training and racing on the track.

Lightweight frame

Nylon pedals with no grips or clips to scratch you in a fall.

Knobbly tyres

Clothing

You need to wear tough, clothing and thick gloves to protect you if you fall off. Strong boots or trainers withstand the rough treatment they receive on corners and protect your feet.

Your body and energy

Different races make different energy demands on you. Your body mainly uses two systems to convert the food you eat into energy.

The aerobic system needs oxygen to provide a slow release of energy over a long period of time, such as during some stretches of a road race.

The anaerobic system mainly uses stored muscle glycogen. This provides a quick burst of energy for a short period, for instance during a sprint.

Most races demand a combination of both kinds of energy. Proper training stimulates the two energy systems.*

*See pages 72-75 for information about training.

Triathlons and biathlons

A triathlon consists of three different sports: cycling, swimming and running. The course includes all three in continuous sequence. Course lengths vary but the following are recognized standards.

> **Olympic/International standard: swim 1500m, cycle 40km, run 10km.**
>
> **Mini triathlon: swim 500m, cycle 20km, run 5km.**

The season runs through spring and summer. You can save money on entry fees if you are a member of the national triathlon association.

A biathlon (or "run: bike: run" event) might involve 5km running, 30km cycling and another 5km running.

Hill climbs

Hill climbs are short but very gruelling. Races may only last about five minutes but even so, some riders do not make it to the finish. You need to build up your levels of strength over many months of hard training.

It is better to start steadily and finish fast than to go off like a bullet and then collapse half way up. On a hill climb there is no respite from the gradient where you can recover from oxygen debt (see below).

Experiment to find your most powerful position. It is likely to be up out of the saddle, using your arms and upper body to pull on the handlebars. Most people stand nearly all the way up, only sitting down on the lesser gradients for a few brief moments.

Riders start at intervals and race against the clock.

Relax your shoulders and keep your back flat. Hunching up will limit your oxygen intake.

When you stand for more power, grip the brake lever hoods and pull on them.

Hill climbs normally take place towards the end of the summer. They are organized by the national time trials association (see page 93).

Training

Strengthening the heart and lungs increases the amount of oxygen you can take in for aerobic energy production. Interval training (see page 75) helps to improve anaerobic energy production.

Oxygen debt

If you ride up a hill as fast as possible, after a while your legs start to ache unbearably and you gasp uncontrollably. This is because your body cannot take in enough oxygen to remove toxic waste from anaerobic energy production. This condition is known as oxygen debt.

If you slow down or stop, the toxic waste is removed in the bloodstream and your muscles will recover.

Basic fitness

The stronger your heart and lungs are, the more oxygen they can supply to your muscles and the longer you will be able to keep going in a race.

You also need plenty of power which comes from muscular strength and flexibility. The next four pages give you some ideas for how to develop all these aspects of fitness.

Stretching exercises

Gentle stretching helps to make you more supple. It also prepares the body for more strenuous activity and speeds up recovery afterwards. Here are some stretches which you can use as a warm-up before a training run or race.

Points to note

- Make sure you are warm before you start.
- Move slowly and relax into the positions – don't "bounce".
- Stretch carefully. It is not meant to hurt.
- Hold stretches for at least ten seconds.
- Try to stretch daily and after cycling as well as before.

Back of neck stretch

Stand up straight and clasp your hands round the back of your neck. Slowly drop your head forwards bringing your elbows in and bending your knees slightly.

Side stretch

Stand with your feet apart and knees slightly bent. Support your body with your right hand on your hip. Stretch your left arm up and over to the side. Repeat other side.

Thigh stretch

Lie on your left side, supporting your head with your hand. Bend your right leg up and grip your ankle. Ease your leg back and hip forward, keeping your knees together. Repeat other side.

Lower back stretch

Lie on your back and pull both knees into your chest. Hold behind your knees.

Hamstring stretch

From the position above, place both hands behind your left thigh. Lower the other foot to the floor. Straighten your left leg until you feel a slight tension at the back of the leg. Hold the position, then repeat other side.

Calf stretch

Stand up straight and rest your hands against a wall. Step back with your left foot and straighten the leg, bending the right leg slightly. Keep your toes facing forwards. Change legs.

Chest and arm stretch

Kneel with your thighs vertical. Slide your hands along the ground until your nose nearly touches it. Press your shoulders towards the ground and try not to arch your back.

Building stamina

When cycling is not practical or you want some variety, running and swimming are good alternatives. You have to do an aerobic activity steadily for at least 20 minutes, three times a week, before it is effective in building stamina.

Building strength

Cycling uses the quadriceps muscle (at the front of your thigh) and the gluteal group (your buttocks). These must be strong but you also need strength in your upper body. Regular circuit and weight training can help to develop both stamina and strength. Find out about sessions at a sports centre.

Circuit training

Circuit training consists of a series of exercises set up at different stations round a sports hall. Each presents a different task which you perform a number of times. You move from station to station until you have completed the circuit.

Weight training

Weight training should be supervised by a qualified coach. You start with light weights and progress to heavier ones. You need to be given a programme which suits your age and fitness level.

Muscles and how they work

Muscles are made up of many thousands of fibres that can lengthen or shorten depending on the demand placed on them. A muscle contains a mixture of red and white fibres.

Red or slow-twitch fibres work when the demand is slower for longer distance riding. This is aerobic work.

Muscle fibres

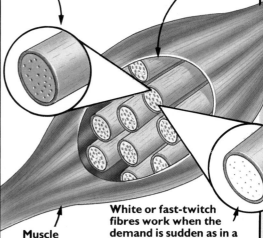

Muscle

White or fast-twitch fibres work when the demand is sudden as in a sprint. This is anaerobic work.

The amount of slow and fast-twitch fibres in a muscle is roughly equal but depends on physical build. If you have more fast-twitch fibres, you may find sprinting and hill-climbs easier than someone with more slow-twitch fibres. They may be able to keep going for longer.

Training on the bike

You are far more likely to achieve success in racing if you put some thought into planning a proper training programme. It is a good idea to record details of your training in a diary. Then when you hit winning form, you can look back to remind yourself how you achieved it.

Warming up

Warming up before a training ride will help your body to benefit. Do a few shoulder rotations and knee lifts followed by some stretches*. Then ride briskly for about 15 minutes before extreme exertion such as sprinting.

Keeping a training diary

Start by testing yourself over about ten kilometres. After warming up take your pulse (see right) and begin your ride. Record the details shown below in your training diary. You can find out how you are improving by testing yourself over the same distance once a month.

Record similar details about all your training rides and also about the other activities included in your programme.

Training diary
Pulse rate- before:
after:
Date:
Time:
Distance:
Weather conditions:
Remarks: (Note how you felt during the ride and how long it took you to recover.)

Pulse rate

When you exert yourself, your muscles need more blood so your heart beats faster. Exercise strengthens your heart so that it pumps out the same amount of blood with fewer beats. This reduces your pulse rate.

Testing your pulse

You need a clock or watch with a second hand.

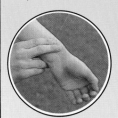

Rest your middle fingers on the inside of your wrist. You should feel a gentle throbbing.

Count how many beats you feel in ten seconds. Multiply this by six. This is your pulse rate per minute.

Finding your training zone

To exercise your heart muscles, you need to raise your pulse to within a training zone. This zone is 65% – 85% of your maximum recommended heart rate during exercise, or MHR. Find your MHR by subtracting your age from 220. This example shows how a 16-year-old would work out his or her training zone.

MHR during exercise: $220 - 16 = 204$

$$\frac{65}{100} \times 204 = 132 \quad \text{(lower end of zone)}$$

$$\frac{85}{100} \times 204 = 173 \quad \text{(upper end of zone)}$$

A 16-year-old's training zone is between 132 and 173 beats per minute. You need to work within your training zone for at least 20 minutes three times a week. Take your pulse immediately after a ride to see if you have been doing so.

Planning a training programme

Below is an outline training programme. It shows when different sorts of exercise are the most useful. How far you should ride and how often depends on your age and fitness, so seek advice from your club coach. In the race season, you can aim to be training or racing six days a week, with one day's rest.

	Preparation	Pre-race	Racing season		Notes
	AUTUMN	**WINTER**	**SPRING**	**SUMMER**	
Stretching exercises	▓▓▓▓▓▓▓▓▓▓▓▓▓▓▓▓▓▓▓▓▓▓▓▓▓				Every day.
Circuit training		▓▓▓▓▓▓▓▓▓▓▓			Leave at least two days between each circuit or weight training session.
Running or swimming		▓▓▓▓▓▓▓▓▓▓▓			
Weight training		▓▓▓▓▓▓▓▓▓▓▓			
Cycle training	▓		▓▓▓▓▓▓▓▓▓▓▓▓▓▓		Build stamina by high winter mileages. Then work on speed in the spring.
Racing	▓	Cyclo-cross	▓▓▓▓▓▓▓▓▓▓		
Monthly mileage	100	80		150	200	

Training on the track

One method of sprint training is to ride 100m fast then 100m slow. This is called interval training. For long distance races, you can increase the distances of speed and recovery to one lap each. Don't exceed six sets per session.

Time trial training

Ride distances of 10-25km (up to 50km as you get fitter) at a steady, fast speed.

Road race training

Steady-state riding (riding at a little harder than an easy pace) and sprinting are good training. Aim to go out twice during the week for between half and one and a half hours, with a longer ride of three or four hours at the weekend.

Group training

Training with other people is more fun and you may find you can achieve more with others to urge you on or compete with. You can practise tactics such as wheel-following and attacking.

Warming down

If you stop exercising suddenly, you may feel faint or get stiff the next day. A warming down session will prevent this. Ride gently for the last 10-15 minutes and then repeat the stretches you did to warm up.*

*See pages 72-73.

75

Cycling kit

The cycling kit shown on this page is specially designed for efficiency, safety, comfort or visibility. You could start with the basics as shown on page 54 and build up your kit as you go along.

Race clothing

For most races, you wear skin-tight cycling jerseys and shorts. There may be rules about the colours you are allowed to wear. An all-in-one skinsuit is an alternative for short races where you don't need pockets to carry food.

Training in the cold

In cold weather, cycling can be a very chilly activity because of the rate at which you move through the air. The effect is similar to standing in a cold wind.

Concentrate on keeping your head and upper body warm. A padded, nylon-fronted jacket will help to keep the wind off.

Your legs tend to stay warmer because they are moving, so a pair of leggings (or tracksuit bottoms tucked into your socks) should be enough.

A racing cape is a type of waterproof jacket. Most are brightly coloured to show up in the rain.

Extra clothes might slow you down a bit but this does not matter for training.

Wear white cotton socks for visibility. Tennis socks with a thick sole and heel are ideal.

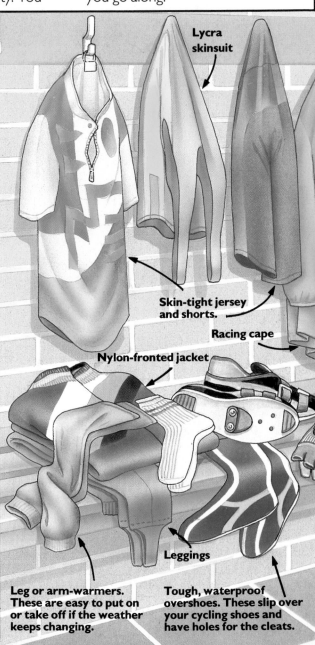

Lycra skinsuit

Skin-tight jersey and shorts.

Racing cape

Nylon-fronted jacket

Leggings

Leg or arm-warmers. These are easy to put on or take off if the weather keeps changing.

Tough, waterproof overshoes. These slip over your cycling shoes and have holes for the cleats.

Clothing accessories

Cycling glasses protect your eyes from dust and grit in the air. Some have lenses which block out harmful ultra-violet light.

A cap shades your eyes – or you can turn it round to shade the back of your neck. It absorbs sweat and you can wear one under a helmet. On its own, though, a cap won't protect you if you fall, so you should only wear one for easy riding on traffic-free roads.

Helmets

When buying a helmet, try it on, tighten the straps and shake your head to make sure it does not slip about on your head. Remember that a helmet will not be effective unless it is secure and done up properly. There are three main types of helmet to choose from, as shown below.

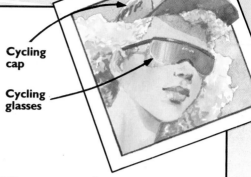

Cycling cap

Cycling glasses

Bike accessories

Cycling water bottles are easy to drink from. The bottle cage attaches to the down tube with metal clips or bottle eyes.

You cannot rely on testing bike light batteries by turning them on since even a dead one might give a short power surge. It is not easy to remember when you last replaced them so carry spares and bulbs.

Banded helmets are comfortable because they are light and airy. You need a good strong one, though.

A soft-shell helmet is made of shock-absorbent polystyrene with a fabric cover. It is light and well-ventilated.

Water bottle and cage

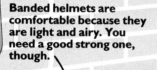

Reflector belts help you to be seen in the dark or the rain.

A hard-shell helmet is made of polystyrene with a rigid cover. It gives good protection but you may need a sweat band as well.

Speedometers

A speedometer, or "computer", helps you to monitor your training progress. It fits on the handlebars and is wired to a sensor on the forks. Generally, the more expensive it is, the more functions it has.

As well as giving your speed and timing your ride, it might show your average speed, maximum speed and mileage, both this trip and since you first used it. Some also show your present and average cadence.

Buying a racing bike

If you want a new bike, you can either buy a complete model or buy a frame and choose components for it separately. (This is more expensive). Cheaper than both is to buy second-hand. A good compromise is to get a good second-hand frame and some new components.

Selecting a frame

A frame is measured by the length of the seat tube. As a rough guide, it should be about 25.5cm less than your inside leg measurement. Good frames are made of butted tubing throughout (see right), such as Reynolds 531 or Columbus SL.

Butted tubing is thinner in the central section and thicker at the joints for strength. It is rigid but light.

Buying a new bike

Even if you are buying a complete bike, the frame is the most important part to get right. You can improve on the components when you can afford to.

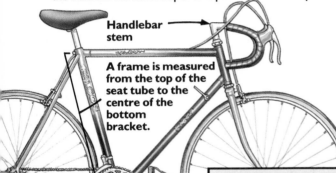

Handlebar stem

A frame is measured from the top of the seat tube to the centre of the bottom bracket.

With about 8cm of seat post exposed, sit on the bike with your foot on the pedal in the downmost position. Your leg should be slightly bent.*

The width of the handlebars should be equal to your shoulder width.

With your elbow touching the point of the saddle, your fingertips should almost reach the handlebars. If they don't, you may need a longer or shorter handlebar stem.

Finding a good shop

You need to find a bike shop that specializes in lightweight racing bikes. A good shop will give you constructive advice and will help to fit you out with a bike that suits your needs, not just one that they want to sell. Ask other cyclists for recommendations and visit a few shops, looking out for the following:

★ A good range of frames and complete bikes plus a variety of components.
★ Helpful assistants who answer people's enquiries intelligently.
★ A workshop repair service and guarantee arrangements.

Buying second-hand

A new bike loses up to a quarter of its value when first ridden, so buying second-hand can be good value. First check the bike fits you (see previous page) and then check the following.

Make sure it is designed for racing (see pages 52-53 and 84-85).

Look for good quality tubing. To check that it is butted, flick it with your fingernail. The note should change as you move away from the joints.

If the bike has been in an accident, the frame might be bent or weakened. Check for dents behind the headset on the down tube and top tube.

Spin the wheels to see if they run straight, checking from the front and the side. Support your finger on a chainstay or fork and hold it against the rim as a guide.

Check for dents in the rims. Check that the spokes are taut. Saggy or bent spokes will need replacing.

Where to look

★ Bike shops which deal in used bikes or frames.
★ The classified pages in cycling magazines.
★ Your club noticeboard. Keen cyclists often change their bikes and equipment.
★ Advertisements in bike shop windows.

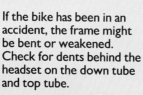

The pedals should be at right angles to the cranks.

Check that the teeth on the chainwheels and sprockets are not worn where they pull on the chain.

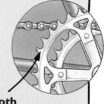

Worn tooth

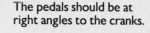

The forks should be in line with the head tube. Look from the side to check. It helps to hold something straight like a ruler up against them.

Take someone more experienced along to check the bike before you hand over any money. If the bike needs new parts, estimate the total cost of the bike and the new parts. Compare this with the price of a new, similar bike to see if the asking price is a fair one.

Trying a bike out

Trying more than one bike is a useful comparison. Make sure you get the saddle and handlebars adjusted to fit you before you start.

★ Check the brakes work smoothly and quickly.
★ Try the gears to make sure they change easily.
★ The bike should ride in a straight line if you take your hands off the bars.
★ Make sure the bike fits you and gives you a comfortable ride.

Looking after your bike

To get the best from your bike, you need to keep it clean and in good running order. At the bottom of the next page are some things you should check each time you set out to ensure that it is safe to ride.

Cleaning the bike

After a ride, wipe any water or sweat off the frame. Sweat is very corrosive.

The bike needs a thorough clean at least once a month. This lengthens the life of its components and gives you a chance to check for worn parts. If you use barrier cream on your hands when cleaning the bike, it is easier to get the dirt and grease off them afterwards. Wear rubber gloves when using strong chemicals.

You will need:
A bucket of warm, soapy water
A soft brush
Rags for drying
An old toothbrush
Degreasing agent (or white spirit)
Light oil or spray lubricant
Rubber gloves and barrier cream
Car wax polish
Chrome polish
An old paint tin or jam jar

Supporting the bike

It is easier to clean or make adjustments to the bike if it is supported on a repair stand. If you don't have one, you can improvise by hanging the frame from a washing line.

Repair stand

Take the wheels out and use a stick to hold the chain in place as shown.

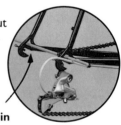

The stick goes through the holes in the seat stays.

Cleaning procedure

Wearing rubber gloves, use an old toothbrush to clean the sprockets, chainwheels, derailleur and brake mechanisms with some degreasing agent. (Pour some into a jam jar or paint tin.) Using a soft brush, wash the frame and wheels in soapy water, starting at the top and working down. Rinse all parts in clean water and dry them thoroughly with a rag.

Use a rag dampened with degreasing agent to clean the chain. Hold the rag over the chain and, with your other hand, turn the cranks anticlockwise. Let the chain run through the rag for several turns. If the chain is very dirty, remove it with a chain tool as follows.

Put the chain in the end slot of the tool and line up the point with one of the rivets. Turn the tool lever clockwise until the point of the tool touches the rivet. Keep turning to drive the rivet just far enough to free the inner link. Don't push the rivet right out as this makes it very difficult to reconnect the chain. Soak the chain in some degreasing agent for a few hours. Hang it up to dry before replacing it.

Point of chain tool pushes rivet out of inner link.

Lubricating and polishing

After cleaning, you need to lubricate the bike with either light oil or spray lubricant. Wipe off any excess, especially from the outside of the chain, and keep it away from brake blocks and wheel rims.

Rub in some wax polish to protect the frame but be careful to keep it off the wheel rims. You can protect the rims and cranks with chrome polish but wear rubber gloves when using it.

Tilt the rear wheel away from you. Run some oil into the freewheel mechanism and over the sprockets.

Lubricate the derailleur at the points where the mechanism pivots.

Lubricate the roller (jockey) wheels where they run on their axles.

Lubricate the front changer at the four points where it pivots, at the pivot bolts.

With the back wheel on, lubricate each chain link. Turn the pedals anticlockwise to move the chain.

Lubricate the gear cables wherever they emerge from the outer housing.

Lubricate the brake calipers at the pivot bolts and where they run against the springs.

Lubricate the brake cables wherever they emerge from the outer housing.

Before you ride

Check the following before a ride.

★ Examine the tyres and remove any foreign bodies, such as grit or glass, with a pair of tweezers.
★ Repair any small cuts in the tyres with fast-acting glue. You will need to let them down to do this.
★ If there is any movement when you pull the brake levers on fully and push forwards, you need to adjust the brakes (see page 83).

★ Pump the tyres up fully: the correct pressure should be printed on the tyre wall. Use a tyre pressure gauge to measure this, as shown in the picture.
★ Check any quick-release levers are closed.

Pressure gauge fits over tyre valve.

Dial shows tyre pressure.

Basic maintenance

Parts wear out or work loose very gradually, so you should establish a routine for checking them regularly.

Brakes need checking weekly and the parts mentioned below at least every three months.

Crank bolts

About once a month, you should check that your crank bolts are tight.

You need an extractor tool that fits your type of crank, and an adjustable spanner.

Remove the dust cap. Position the spanner end of the tool over the crank bolt. Place the adjustable spanner over the tool and turn it clockwise to tighten the bolt. Hold the crank steady with your other hand.

Adjustable spanner

Crank bolt　　　**Extractor tool**

Gears

To stop the chain jumping off the sprockets or chainwheels when you change into top or bottom gear, you need to adjust the derailleur or the front changer mechanisms.

Locate the high and low adjusting screws. These limit the range of movement of the derailleur or front changer. With a small screwdriver, adjust a screw half a turn at a time and check the gears again.

Adjusting screws on derailleur.　　　**Adjusting screws on front changer.**

Hub adjustment

Hubs, like other moving parts, contain bearings which need occasional adjustment. Correct adjustment means that the wheel turns freely and smoothly and there is no play when you hold the axle and wiggle the wheel from side to side.

To adjust a front hub, take the wheel out of the frame. Use a cone spanner and an adjustable spanner for the job.

Hold the cone with the cone spanner as you loosen the locknut with the adjustable spanner. Remove the washer. Turn the cone an eighth to a quarter of a turn (clockwise to tighten, anticlockwise to loosen).* Hold the cone in place as you retighten the locknut. If the hub does not turn smoothly when adjusted, the hub bearings, cones or axle may need replacing (see page 84).

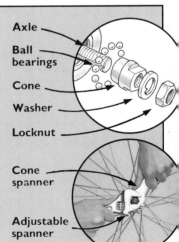

Axle

Ball bearings

Cone

Washer

Locknut

Cone spanner

Adjustable spanner

*It is important not to tighten or loosen the cones too much as this can damage the bearings.

Brakes

If there is more than 5cm of movement at the brake levers between the off and on positions, loosen the locknut on the calipers. Then screw up the adjuster anticlockwise. If it is as far as it will go, you need to tighten the cable as follows.

Screw the adjuster right down (clockwise) and with a small spanner loosen the cable anchor bolt. Press the calipers together as you pull the cable down and retighten the bolt. You need more than two hands to do this, so ask someone to help.

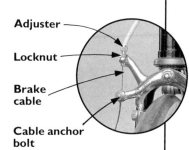

Adjuster

Locknut

Brake cable

Cable anchor bolt

Check that each brake block strikes the wheel rim and not the tyre itself.

At the same time, check the blocks for wear and replace both blocks even if only one is worn.

To adjust or replace a block, undo the acorn nut at the side of the calipers with a spanner. Apply the brake, hold the block in position and tighten the nut. Make sure the block is facing the right way. Most have an arrow and the word "forwards" imprinted in the rubber.

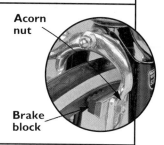

Acorn nut

Brake block

The blocks should spring clear of the rims when you release the levers. If they stick or are slow to react, the calipers may be poorly lubricated, or you may need to adjust the pivot bolt as follows.

With a small spanner, loosen first the locknut (if there is one) and then the adjusting nut in front very slightly.*

Retighten the locknut and check the brakes again.

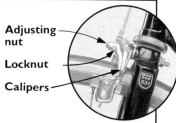

Adjusting nut

Locknut

Calipers

The brake levers should be firmly fixed to the bars. If they are loose, tighten the bolt inside the brake lever. You will need either a screwdriver or an allen key to do this.

First, loosen the cable anchor bolt to release the cable. Pull on the brake levers and pull the cable aside. You will then be able to get to the bolt to tighten it.

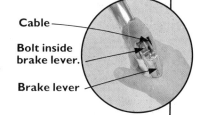

Cable

Bolt inside brake lever.

Brake lever

At the same time, check for fraying brake cables, especially at the cable anchor bolt and inside the brake lever.

Replace the cables if any strands are broken.

If your bike has concealed cables (aero levers), release the cable at the anchor bolt. Push the end of the cable up as far as the adjuster and pull on the brake lever. The cable will protrude from the lever.

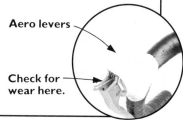

Aero levers

Check for wear here.

---

*Be careful not to loosen the pivot bolt too much or the calipers will rock forwards as you brake.

Maintaining bearings

The moving parts of a bike – the hubs*, bottom bracket, headset and pedals – all contain bearings. If the bearings are not properly adjusted they wear unevenly and damage the component. As well as checking the adjustment every so often, the ball bearings should be replaced and lubricated every three to six months.

Some bikes contain bearings in a sealed unit which does not need overhauling. Good ones may take up to ten years to wear out. Then you need to replace the whole unit.

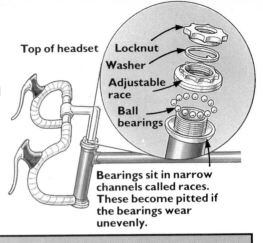

Top of headset

Locknut

Washer

Adjustable race

Ball bearings

Bearings sit in narrow channels called races. These become pitted if the bearings wear unevenly.

Annual overhauling

You should give your bike a thorough overhaul every year before the race season. This involves dismantling it completely so that you can clean, lubricate and replace parts if necessary.

There is not enough space in this book to describe how to do this but the list on the right gives you an idea of what needs to be done. Ask an experienced person to help you, or buy or borrow a good bike maintenance book.

★ Bottom bracket. Dismantle down to the spindle. Check for pitting and wear from contact with the bearings.
★ Gears. Replace the cables as they stretch and rust over time. Check the alignment of the gear mechanisms (see page 82).
★ Headset. Dismantle it to check the bearings (see top of page). Replace any damaged or corroded parts.
★ Brakes. Replace the brake cables. Run through all the checks on page 83.
★ Wheels and hubs. Check the hub bearings. Check the spokes for damage and replace if necessary. See that the spokes are tight and that the wheels run true (straight).
★ Chain and chainwheels. Replace the chain if you can lift it more than 3mm off the chainwheels. Check for worn or bent chainwheel teeth.
★ Seatpin and handlebar stem. Remove these (see below) and grease them lightly to stop them rusting into position.

Saddle and handlebar adjustments

To remove, raise or lower the saddle, loosen the seat bolt using either a spanner or an allen key. To move the saddle backwards or forwards, loosen nuts A and B. (On some bikes, you loosen the bolt under the top of the seat post.)

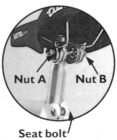

Nut A   **Nut B**

Seat bolt

To remove, raise or lower the handlebars, loosen the expander bolt on top of the stem. Tap the top sharply to release the wedge inside. To change the angle of the bars, loosen bolt A. Do all bolts up tightly after adjustment.**

Expander bolt

Bolt A

*See page 82 for how to adjust the hub bearings.
**You should check seat and handlebar bolts are tight every few weeks.

Club cycling

As a member of a cycling club, you are more likely to get a place in local or national races and build up your racing experience. The club coach can help you to choose races and set objectives. You can also pick up tactics and techniques from more experienced members.

Finding a club

A bike shop may be able to give you details of local cycling clubs. Otherwise, contact the national cycling federation (address on page 93). Try to find out how the local clubs differ. Here are some questions you may want to ask about them.

1. What sort of cycling are most members interested in? Don't join a touring club if you want to race.

2. Is the club affiliated to the national cycling federation and time trials council? This will enable you to enter national events.

3. Does the club coach organize any winter training such as weight and circuit training?

4. Does the club have a sponsor who gives some financial support? This might cover transport to races and some equipment.

Chain gangs

Groups of riders, often from more than one club, may meet up and race against one another in mock competition. These are called chain gangs. If you get the chance, join one a little above your standard so that you are stretched but still able to keep up and take your turn at the front. Chain gangs tend to be hard rides rather than gentle runs and are therefore good race practice.

Entering races

Cycle races are usually promoted by local clubs or national federations. Entry forms should be sent in at least three weeks in advance to be sure of getting a place.* (Your club secretary will have a supply of standard forms.) For road races, you also need a race licence which you buy from the cycling federation. It lasts for a year.

About a week before the race you should receive course details and a list of competitors. These will help you to plan your race tactics. For a time trial, you will also receive a starting time.

On the day of the race, try to arrive about an hour before the start (a little less for time trials). You then need to report to the following people:

The **examiner** checks your bike and gives you an examination ticket if he is satisfied that it is in good working order.**

The **licence steward** takes your examination ticket and race licence and gives you a race number to wear.

The **chief commissaire** then calls all the riders together (either in the changing room or at the start line) to warn them of any dangers on the route or any changes that have had to be made due to hazards such as floods.

After the race, the **chief judge** will tell you your placing in the race and whether you have scored any points.

Collect your race licence from the licence steward. The chief commissaire then makes a note in it of any points gained. This is called endorsing your licence.

*You can normally enter club time trials and cyclo-cross races on the day.
**This only applies to road races and criteriums.

Design and technology

Basic bike design has changed little since the 1900s. However, the development of lightweight materials, such as aluminium alloys and carbon fibre, has improved its efficiency. The bike on the opposite page shows some recent design innovations.

Frame geometry

As you pedal, you exert a force on one side of the bike and then the other. This makes the frame bend slightly, using up energy. Energy loss is reduced on a racing bike by making the frame stiffer.

Increasing the angles shown on the diagram and shortening the chainstays makes the frame shorter and therefore stiffer.

On a racing bike the angle between the seat tube and top tube is normally between 73° and 75°.

Shorter chainstays than on touring bike.

On a touring bike, the angle is normally 72° or 73°.

Forks

The steeper and straighter the forks, the more responsive the bike will be to small movements.

Increasing the angle marked at the top of the fork diagram makes them steeper. The amount the forks bend at the bottom is called the fork rake. On a racing bike, the fork rake is usually 5cm or less.

Fork rake

Disc wheels

As the spokes go round on a normal wheel, they catch the air and slow you down. Disc wheels reduce this effect as the air flows smoothly over the disc's surface. However, bikes are often only fitted with a rear disc: a front disc makes the bike difficult to steer in a sidewind because air cannot pass through it.

The best discs are light carbon fibre and are very expensive. Plastic or fabric clip-on covers are a cheaper alternative.

The *Union Cycliste Internationale* (UCI) which sets the standards for all races does not allow aerodynamic attachments. Disc wheels are permitted as they are part of the bike. Clip-on wheel covers are illegal.

Index gears

On ordinary (open) gears, you judge the movement of the shift lever by feel or ear. With an index system, you move the lever until it clicks into a position that lines the derailleur up with the sprocket automatically. This is done by means of stops inside the lever mechanism.

Expensive index systems can be changed to the ordinary system by a switch on the side of the lever.

Aerodynamics

As you ride, your effort is going into overcoming friction. There is friction between the road and your wheels (called rolling resistance), between the moving parts of your bike, and between the air and your body and bike (called aerodynamic drag).

As you pick up speed, you fight aerodynamic drag more than anything else. Some things help to reduce this, such as a streamlined position, skin-tight clothing and certain design features such as disc wheels.

Handlebar extensions

Handlebar extensions, sometimes called aero bars, give you the option of a very streamlined position. They clamp on to your existing bars with allen key bolts.*

Oval chainwheels

Oval (elliptical) chainwheels have the effect of slightly changing gear as you pedal. This means that when your cranks are horizontal and you are able to push your hardest, you are in a larger gear. However, elliptical chainwheels can also interfere with the development of a smooth pedalling style.

Specialized bikes

Although standard racing bikes have not changed much, there have been some specialist developments which improve speed or performance in certain events.

Low profile bikes

Low profile bikes are generally used in time trials. The front wheel is smaller, the head tube short and the bars shaped upwards and forwards to give a very low riding position. In some cases the seat tube is curved to allow the back wheel to come in closer. This is the ultimate racing bike for combatting aerodynamic drag and improving speed.

The front wheel has fewer spokes than usual for lightness.

Mountain bikes

Mountain bikes were first designed for racing off-road and they are often seen in cyclo-cross races. Three chainwheels provide gears low enough for steep, broken ground. Because of the comfortable riding position, they are also popular with city riders.

Straight handlebars for a comfortable position.

Thick, knobbly tyres for rough ground. →

Recumbent bikes

The rider pedals a recumbent bike from a low, reclined position. The aerodynamic drag is 20% less than on an upright bicycle. The UCI does not allow them in any of their races but enthusiasts organize their own races.

The recumbent position supports the rider so that the whole effort goes into pedalling.

*Handlebar extensions are illegal in some races.

Safety on the bike

Although crashes and falls are not always avoidable, riding safely may help prevent them. Just like any other road user, you must be familiar with the rules of the road and consider other vehicles.

Traffic and other hazards

Although bikes have the same rights as other vehicles, as a cyclist you are more vulnerable. Make sure all your signals are clear and be definite and confident in your movements. The following points are relevant to bike riding in general, not specifically race training.

★ Many cities have marked cycle paths. Take advantage of these if there are any along your route.

★ Obey all traffic signs and signals. Be ready to stop at pedestrian crossings.

★ Check behind before pulling out to pass a parked vehicle. Remember that the driver may open the door in your path.

★ If you have to cross the path of vehicles behind in order to turn off the road, look back well in advance to check when it will be safe to move across. Signal clearly and check again before you manoeuvre.

★ Except in very slow traffic, leave at least three bicycle lengths between you and the vehicle ahead in case it stops suddenly or turns in front of you.

★ Exhaust fumes from heavy traffic are very unhealthy. Wearing a mask can help or better still, look for alternative back roads.

★ Ride far enough away from the edge of the road to avoid drains and gutters.

★ Colourful clothing and a reflector band enable drivers to see you from much further away than without them. Use reflectors and lights in dull weather as well as at night.

★ Keep your eyes on the road. To check behind, it is quicker and easier to duck your head down rather than twist it to the side.

★ You will find it easier to accelerate out of sticky situations if you are in a medium gear in which you can speed up without too much effort.

★ Before stopping, look behind and come to a halt slowly. Unless in an emergency, never surprise riders or drivers behind by skidding to a halt.

★ On country roads, give horses and other animals a very wide berth. It is better to keep pedalling as the clicking noise of the freewheel may frighten the animal.

★ Bear in mind that, early or late in the day, drivers may be blinded by a low sun and miss seeing you altogether.

The highway code

If you are unfamiliar with the highway code, it would be a good idea to buy or borrow a copy from your local library. It explains the rules of the road and the signs which you need to be able to recognize. All road users are supposed to know the highway code.

You may find a national cycling proficiency scheme useful even if you are quite an experienced cyclist. These train you to recognize and avoid risky situations and to cycle according to the highway code. The courses usually only last a couple of days and are free.

Crashes

In races and when you are training at high speeds, falls and collisions can happen so fast that there is little time to avoid them. The best you can do is to be alert and try to anticipate danger by keeping your eyes on the road ahead. Below are some situations in which you need to take special care.

Riding in a bunch

Leave at least 15cm between your front wheel and the back wheel of the rider in front. If your wheels touch, you will be thrown violently over the handlebars.

The leaders of a bunch should warn of any danger in the road. They should point to an obstacle such as a pothole as they pass it and you should do the same to those behind you.

Bumpy roads

On bumpy roads, sit back on the saddle and hold the tops of the bars, with your elbows well bent. Look out for cracks or ridges in the road. If you hit one at speed, it can throw you sideways. If you spot it in time, try using the avoidance technique described on page 58.

Slippery surfaces

To avoid skidding on wet, oily or leaf-strewn surfaces, sit as upright as you can. Shift your weight back, don't rise off the saddle and avoid any sudden movements or hard braking.

Steep hills

It is easy to lose control of the steering when you are speeding downhill. Try to stay relaxed and in command by gripping the handlebars firmly and leaning into corners. Also, beware of loose chippings and leaves that gather at the bottom of hills. You can easily skid on these if you hit them at speed, especially if you are trying to corner at the same time.

Finishing a race

The elation of finishing a race makes it easy to lose concentration, especially if you are first over the line. Don't take your focus off the road ahead until you have come to a halt. Take care when turning round that you don't collide with other riders crossing the line.

Injuries

Deal with any injury as soon as possible. Cuts and grazes should be cleaned with warm water and some sort of antiseptic cream or lotion. Then cover the area to protect it from dust and dirt. Bruises can be treated with an ice pack** (a bag of frozen peas is ideal).

Press the ice pack gently against the bruised area for about 20 minutes.

Put a thin towel between the skin and the ice pack to avoid ice burn.

Falling off

Here are some ways in which you may be able to reduce the injury if you do fall.

★ Wear a good helmet.*
★ Relax your arms and legs to absorb the shock of a fall.
★ Wear gloves (track mitts) to save your hands from being grazed.

★ As you fall, curl up and try to go into a roll to absorb the shock. Tuck your head in and fold your arms round it.

---

*More about helmets on page 77.
**See page 30 for how to make an ice pack.

Cycling injuries

At one time or another, you may be unlucky enough to suffer from cycling-induced injuries or conditions such as those listed below. Here are some suggestions for prevention and treatment.

Cramp

Cramp in a calf muscle is often the result of insufficient training or not warming up properly. Pre-race massage can help to prepare your muscles against cramp. After a ride, massage helps to free the muscles. If you get cramp on a ride, try pushing your heels hard down as you pedal or stop and relax the muscle.

To relieve cramp, try pressing hard into the thickest part of the muscle and hold for a count of ten. The pain should gradually ease.

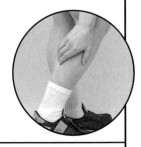

Saddle sores

The chamois or synthetic padded insert in cycling shorts helps to prevent chaffing of the groin area as long as the insert is worn directly next to the skin. Wash your shorts after each wearing with a gentle soap powder that won't destroy the chamois.

You can buy chamois creams which you rub into the insert as added prevention to chaffing. If you get saddle sores, avoid using soap but bathe the area with warm water and a hypo-allergenic cleanser for sensitive skin. If possible, stop riding for a while to let the sores heal.

Numb hands or feet

If you suffer from numb hands, try shifting their position on the handlebars more often. Padded cycling gloves (track mitts) help as they absorb some vibration from the road. Numb feet may result from your toe straps being too tight. System pedals are more comfortable as they work without toe straps.

System pedals have quick-release bindings that grip the soles of your shoes very tightly. You don't need toeclips.

Knee and other joint problems

Pain in your knees, lower back or shoulders may be due to an incorrect position on the bike. The riding position should never fully extend the legs, arms or back. Knee problems can start if your foot is misaligned on the pedal. Try adjusting the cleats, or your shoeplates if you have system pedals.

After a ride

Even on a hot day, put on some extra clothing and warm down after a ride. As soon as you can, have a shower. This is relaxing and rejuvenating and helps to fend off stiffness.

When not to ride

A rise in body temperature or normal pulse rate* are indications that you are unwell and should not exert yourself. As you recover, revert to training at a low level and build up slowly.

Food and nutrition

Cycling demands a lot of energy from your body. The main energy source in food is carbohydrate but proteins, fats, vitamins and minerals are also essential nutrients. A healthy diet might include a variety of the foods in the chart below although the highest percentage should be in the form of carbohydrates.

Nutrients	Good sources	Uses in the body
Carbohydrates	Cereals, bread, rice, potatoes, pasta, pulses.	These are the primary fuel source. Brown or wholemeal varieties contain more fibre which helps the food pass through the digestive system.
Fats	Vegetable oils, margarine, peanut butter, full-fat milk, cheese, butter.	During prolonged exercise, fats can be used as energy fuel. An excess is stored as body fat. Vegetable fat is better for you than animal fat.
Proteins	Dairy products, meat, fish, pulses, nuts, seeds.	Proteins are essential for growth and the repair of damaged body tissue.
Vitamins and minerals	Fresh fruit and vegetables.	These are vital for the regulation of body processes.

Eating for the race

Your last big meal should be at least three hours before the race. Otherwise, you may suffer from dreadful stomach cramps during the race. This is because your digestive system may be starved of the energy it needs to digest the meal. Instead, the energy is being diverted to your muscles.

It is a good idea to make this last big meal dinner the night before the race. Try to eat plenty of carbohydrate as this will constitute your source of energy for the race.

Breakfast

On the morning of the race, have a moderately-sized, carbohydrate-based breakfast and a hot drink.

During the race

You can carry water on any race if you think you might want a drink. In races over 40km you will certainly need one.*

Instead of water you could take an energy drink. This tops up your fluid level when you are working energetically and sweating. It replaces lost glucose, salts and minerals and is easily absorbed.

In a race over 75km, you will also need food to replenish your energy supplies. Malt loaf, fruit and muesli bars are easily digested and satisfy your stomach.**

After the race

Round the day off with a carbohydrate-based meal and plenty of fluid. Eat plenty of protein the following day.

*Water flavoured with fruit juice is ideal.
**More about race food on page 61.

Gear restrictions

In some races, there is a maximum gear restriction to prevent riders straining in too high a gear and damaging their muscles and joints. Because the same gear makes different-sized wheels travel different distances, the maximum gear is measured by the distance travelled per crank revolution.

You can get details of gear restrictions from your club or cycling federation. To check your own top gear, consult a table such as the one below or work it out as. shown.

Using a gear table

Find the sprocket and chainwheel size of your highest gear on the table. Where the sprocket column meets the chainwheel row is the distance covered per crank revolution. This table is for standard sprint rims with normal road tubular tyres and 700c* rims with racing tyres.

Adjusting the gears

If your highest gear exceeds the gear restriction, you need to adjust the derailleur mechanism so that it does not move the chain on to the smallest sprocket. You can find out how to make this adjustment on page 82.

Gear table

CHAIN-WHEEL SIZE	SPROCKET SIZE														
	12	13	14	15	16	17	18	19	20	21	22	23	24	25	26
40	7·01	6·47	6·01	5·61	5·26	4·95	4·67	4·42	4·20	4·00	3·82	3·66	3·50	3·36	3·23
41	7·19	6·63	6·16	5·75	5·39	5·07	4·79	4·53	4·31	4·10	3·92	3·75	3·59	3·44	3·31
42	7·36	6·79	6·31	5·89	5·52	5·19	4·90	4·65	4·41	4·20	4·01	3·84	3·68	3·53	3·39
43	7·54	6·96	6·46	6·03	5·65	5·32	5·02	4·76	4·52	4·30	4·11	3·93	3·77	3·61	3·47
44	7·71	7·12	6·61	6·17	5·78	5·44	5·14	4·87	4·63	4·40	4·20	4·02	3·85	3·70	3·56
45	7·89	7·28	6·76	6·31	5·91	5·57	5·26	4·98	4·73	4·50	4·30	4·11	3·94	3·78	3·64
46	8·06	7·44	6·91	6·45	6·04	5·69	5·37	5·09	4·84	4·60	4·39	4·21	4·03	3·86	3·72
47	8·24	7·60	7·06	6·59	6·18	5·81	5·49	5·20	4·94	4·70	4·49	4·30	4·12	3·95	3·80
48	8·42	7·77	7·21	6·73	6·31	5·94	5·61	5·31	5·05	4·80	4·59	4·39	4·20	4·03	3·88
49	8·59	7·93	7·36	6·87	6·44	6·06	5·72	5·42	5·15	4·91	4·68	4·48	4·29	4·12	3·96
50	8·77	8·09	7·51	7·01	6·57	6·19	5·84	5·53	5·26	5·01	4·78	4·57	4·38	4·20	4·04
51	8·94	8·25	7·66	7·15	6·70	6·31	5·96	5·64	5·36	5·11	4·87	4·66	4·47	4·28	4·12
52	9·12	8·41	7·81	7·29	6·83	6·43	6·07	5·75	5·47	5·21	4·97	4·75	4·56	4·37	4·20
53	9·29	8·58	7·96	7·43	6·96	6·56	6·19	5·86	5·57	5·31	5·06	4·84	4·62	4·45	4·28
54	9·47	8·74	8·11	7·57	7·10	6·68	6·31	5·97	5·68	5·41	5·16	4·94	4·73	4·54	4·36
55	9·64	8·90	8·26	7·71	7·23	6·80	6·42	6·08	5·78	5·51	5·25	5·03	4·82	4·62	4·45
56	9·82	9·06	8·41	7·85	7·36	6·93	6·54	6·19	5·89	5·61	5·35	5·12	4·91	4·70	4·53

Measuring the distance

With the cranks vertical, mark the ground directly below. Move the bike back for one revolution of the crank and draw another mark. The distance between the marks is the distance travelled per crank revolution. Alternatively, you can work the distance out as follows.

Divide the number of chainwheel teeth by the sprocket teeth. Multiply by 3.142 (known as pi). Multiply by the diameter of the wheel. For example:

Chainwheel

$$\frac{52}{17} \times 3{\cdot}142 \times 0{\cdot}67m = 6{\cdot}44m$$

Sprocket   Pi   Wheel diameter   Distance

Useful addresses

To find out more about cycling events or clubs in your area, you can contact your country's national cycling federation. You probably need to belong to the federation to enter certain races and some have facilities such as automatic insurance against bike accidents.

International

Union Cycliste Internationale (UCI)
6 Rue Amat
1202 Genève
Switzerland

Great Britain

British Cycling Federation
36 Rockingham Road
Kettering
Northamptonshire
NN16 8HG

Tel. 0536-412211

Road Time Trials Council
Dallacre House
Mill Road
Yarwell
Peterborough
PE8 6PS

Tel. 0780-782464

British Cyclo-Cross Association
59 Jordan Road
Sutton Coldfield
West Midlands
B75 5AE

Tel. 021-308-1246

Cycle Speedway Council
57 Rectory Lane
Poringland
Norwich
NR14 7SW

Tel. 05086-3880

British Triathlon Association
(Junior Team Manager)
4 Tynemouth Terrace
Tynemouth
NE30 4BH

Tel. 091-258-1438

USA

United States Cycling Federation
1750 East Boulder Street
Colorado Springs
CO 80909

Tel. 719-578-4581

Canada

Canadian Cycling Association
1600 Prom. James Naismith Dr.
Gloucester
Ontario
K1B 5N4

Tel. 613-748-5629

Australia

Australian Cycling Federation
68 Broadway
Sydney
NSW 2007

Tel. 02-281-8688

Australian Cycle Speedway Council
National Secretary
7 Broadford Crescent
Findon
South Australia 5023

Tel. 618 347 0655

New Zealand

New Zealand Amateur Cycling Association
PO Box 35-048
Christchurch

Tel. 03-851-422

Ireland

Federation of Irish Cycling
Halston Street
Dublin 7

Tel. 01-727524

Glossary

Aerobic activity An activity which relies on an energy system that uses oxygen to supply energy over a long period of time.

Aerodynamic drag The slowing down effect of the air on your body and bike as you ride.

Anaerobic activity An activity which relies on an energy system that uses stored muscle glycogen to give you a quick burst of energy.

Ankling A technique which increases pedalling power. You change the angle of your foot in order to pull up on the toeclips as well as push down on the pedals.

Attacking Making a calculated move to break away from a **bunch** in a race in order to gain a lead or split up the race.

Banking The ends of a cycle track which slope upwards to prevent the riders slipping as they speed round the bends.

Biathlon An event consisting of both cycling and running, sometimes called "run:bike:run" event.

Bit and bit A technique where riders in a group take turns to lead in order to share the effort and keep up the pace.

Break A rider or group of riders who pull away from a **bunch** in a race.

Bunch The main group of riders in a race.

Butted tubing Good-quality frame tubing which is thinner in the central section and thicker at the joints to make the frame rigid but light.

Cadence The rate at which your pedals go round measured in revolutions per minute (revs or rpm).

Chain-gang A group of riders from different clubs who meet for training runs.

Cleat A shoe plate that screws on to the sole of a cycling shoe and slots on to the edge of the pedal. It keeps the foot in position on the pedal.

Cone spanner A very thin spanner that fits the hub cones.

Criterium A type of **road race** that takes place on a closed circuit free from traffic, such as a park. Riders have to lap the circuit a set number of times.

Cycle speedway A fast and furious cycle sport that takes place on special shale tracks.

Cyclo-cross A winter sport that combines cycling with running and sometimes carrying the bike over obstacles and rough ground.

Disc wheel A type of wheel with flat surfaces instead of spokes, used to reduce the effects of **aerodynamic drag**.

Echelon A staggered line of riders. Riders position themselves slightly behind and either to the right or left of the rider in front in order to shelter from a sidewind.

Embrocation A type of oil used by cyclists. Applied lightly to the skin, it helps to keep the body warm.

Energy drink A preparation that you buy in powder form and mix with water. As a drink on long races or rides, it replaces lost glucose, salts and minerals as well as fluid.

Field Collective term for all the riders in a race.

Handicap race An event in which riders from different categories start at different times. This gives lower category riders a head start.

Handsling A technique used in a team **track race** to propel your partner into the race.

High-pressure tyre A type of tyre that has an inner tube, used on racing and touring bikes.

Hill climb A short gruelling race against the clock up a very steep hill.

Honking   Rising from the saddle to a standing position and using your body weight to increase the pressure on the pedals as you climb a steep hill.

Index gearing   A gear system with a mechanism in the gear lever. As you move the lever, it clicks into position automatically.

Madison   A team **track race** where the two riders in each team take turns to race for a certain distance.

Massed start event   A **road race** in which all riders start together.

Oxygen debt   A condition which can develop when you are riding hard. Your muscles start to burn or ache because your body cannot take in enough oxygen to remove toxic waste from anaerobic energy production.

Peloton   The French word for **bunch**.

Pressure gauge   A device that you can slot on to the tyre valve which registers the air pressure in the tyre.

Primes   (pronounced preem) Interim targets to aim for during a **road race** where you can win extra points or prizes.

Pursuit   A **track race** where two riders start at opposite sides of the track and try to catch each other up.

Randonnée   A non-competitive ride over a varying distance (from 50km up to 1000km).

Reliability ride   See **randonnée**.

Road race   A race held on the open road. Distances vary from 40km to over 100km. There are no road races for Juveniles.

Rolling resistance   The friction between your bike tyres and the road surface as you ride.

Scratch race   A **massed start road race** where all categories ride the same distance.

Skinsuit   An all-in-one garment usually made of lycra. These are often worn in track or short-distance events where pockets are not needed for carrying food.

Slipstreaming   Riding directly behind another rider in order to travel as fast but with less effort.

Speedometer   A small gadget sometimes called a bike computer, that fits on to the handlebars. It has a sensor attached to the forks and might show **cadence** as well as mileage and speed.

Stage race   A long **road race** such as the *Tour de France* or the British Milk Race. Each day (or stage) is a separate race with its own prizes. At the end, each rider's time for all stages are totalled. The shortest overall time wins.

System pedals   An alternative to normal pedals and toeclips. Shoe-plates fitted to the soles of cycling shoes slot into the pedals which have quick-release bindings.

Time trial   A race on the road where riders start at one-minute intervals and race against the clock.

Track mitts   Padded cycling gloves, (often fingerless).

Track race   Any event that takes place on a cycle track such as a sprint, **pursuit** or **madison**.

Triathlon   An event that combines running, cycling and swimming in continuous sequence.

Tubular tyre (tub)   Tubeless tyre used on a sprint rim. It is either cemented to the rim or fixed with double-sided tape.

Tyre pressure   The amount of air pressure in a tyre. It is measured in pounds per square inch (psi) or atmospheres (bars). The recommended amount of air for a tyre is printed on the side of the tyre, in bars or psi.

Wheel-following   See **slipstreaming**.

Index

With thanks to: Robin Kyte, and Fred Williams Cycles Ltd, Wolverhampton.